Ian McPhedran is an award-wi[...]
previous books. Until 2016, he w[...]
for News Limited and during his[...]
he covered conflicts in Myanma., ~omana, Cambodia, Papua
New Guinea, Indonesia, East Timor, Afghanistan and Iraq. In
1993, he won a United Nations Association Peace Media Award
and in 1999 the Walkley Award for Best News Report for his
exposé of the Navy's Collins-class submarine fiasco. McPhedran
lives in Balmain with his wife Verona Burgess.

Also by Ian McPhedran

The Smack Track
Afghanistan: Australia's War
Too Bold to Die
Air Force
Soldiers Without Borders
The Amazing SAS

THE MIGHTY KRAIT

THE LITTLE BOAT THAT PULLED OFF AUSTRALIA'S MOST DARING COMMANDO RAID OF WWII

IAN McPHEDRAN

HarperCollins*Publishers*

In memory of Douglas Herps and Warwick Thomson

HarperCollins_Publishers_

First published in Australia in 2018
by HarperCollins_Publishers_ Australia Pty Limited
ABN 36 009 913 517

harpercollins.com.au

HarperCollins_Publishers_
Level 13, 201 Elizabeth Street, Sydney NSW 2000, Australia
Unit D1, 63 Apollo Drive, Rosedale, Auckland 0632, New Zealand
A 53, Sector 57, Noida, UP, India
1 London Bridge Street, London SE1 9GF, United Kingdom
Bay Adelaide Centre, East Tower, 22 Adelaide Street West, 41st floor, Toronto,
  Ontario M5H 4E3, Canada
195 Broadway, New York NY 10007, USA

A catalogue record for this book is available from the National Library of Australia

ISBN: 978 1 4607 5564 8 (paperback)
ISBN: 978 1 4607 0980 1 (epub)

Cover design by Phil Campbell Design
Cover images: Japanese ship *Sinkoku Maru*. This ship was damaged and set on fire at
Singapore by Major Lyon and A.B. Huston of the operative party of Operation Jaywick,
AWM, 045434; 'Last we Saw of Singapore', Museums Victoria, 1715429
Back cover image by Warren Croser, courtesy *Northern Star*
Maps by Laurie Whiddon, Map Illustrations
Typeset in Bembo Std by Kirby Jones
Printed and bound in Australia by McPhersons Printing Group
The papers used by HarperCollins in the manufacture of this book are a natural,
recyclable product made from wood grown in sustainable plantation forests. The fibre
source and manufacturing processes meet recognised international environmental
standards, and carry certification.

Contents

After Jaywick

Saving the *Krait*

Glossary

2IC	Second in Command
ADF	Australian Defence Force
AIB	Allied Intelligence Bureau
ANMM	Australian National Maritime Museum
AWM	Australian War Memorial
Bulwark	An extension of a boat's sides above deck level
DSC	Distinguished Service Cross
DSO	Distinguished Service Order
Folboat	Folding timber-framed, canvas-covered two-man canoe
Forecastle	The forward deck of a ship
Framing	The structure that gives a vessel its shape
Garboard	The first planks or plates laid next to a vessel's keel
Head	A marine toilet
HMAS	Her (or his) Majesty's Australian Ship
HMB	His (or her) Majesty's Bark

HMS	Her (or his) Majesty's Ship
Hold	A storage area for cargo on a ship
ISD	Inter-allied Services Department
Keel	The main structure along the length of the bottom of a boat
MC	Military Cross
MI5	Great Britain's domestic intelligence service
MI6	Great Britain's overseas intelligence service
MID	Mentioned in Dispatches
MM	Military Medal
MV	Motor Vessel
PTS	Post-traumatic stress
PTSD	Post-traumatic stress disorder
RAAF	Royal Australian Air Force
RAN	Royal Australian Navy
RANVR	Royal Australian Navy Volunteer Reserve
RNR	Royal Navy Reserve
RVCP	Royal Volunteer Coastal Patrol
SAS	Special Air Service Regiment
Sea state	The degree of turbulence at sea according to average wave height
Seine	A fishing net that floats vertically in the water to encircle fish
SOA	Special Operations Australia
SOE	Special Operations Executive
SP	Starting Price
SRD	Services Reconnaissance Department
SS	Steamship
UN	United Nations
USN	United States Navy

USS	United States Ship
VC	Victoria Cross; the highest Imperial/Australian award for valour
ZES	'Z' Experimental Station

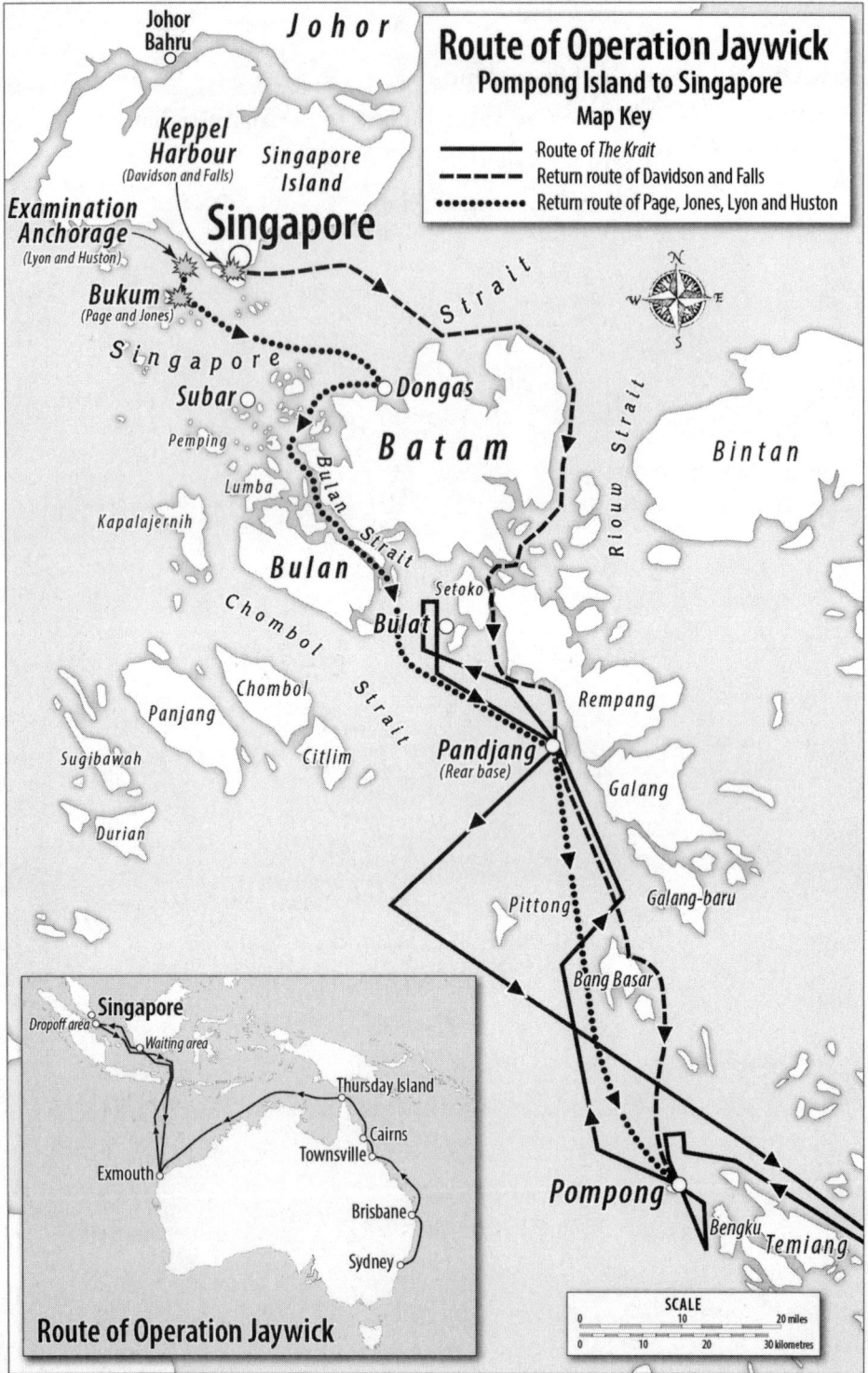

Route of Operation Jaywick
Pompong Island to Singapore
Map Key

— Route of *The Krait*

– – – Return route of Davidson and Falls

••••••• Return route of Page, Jones, Lyon and Huston

Johor Bahru

J o h o r

Keppel
Harbour
(Davidson and Falls)

Singapore Island

Singapore

Examination
Anchorage
(Lyon and Huston)

Bukum
(Page and Jones)

S i n g a p o r e

Strait

Subar

Dongas

Pemping

B a t a m

Bintan

Lumba

Bulan Strait

Kapalajernih

Bulan

Bulat

Setoko

Rempang

Riouw Strait

C h o m b o l

Chombol

Panjang

Citlim

Chombol Strait

Pandjang
(Rear base)

Galang

Sugibawah

Pittong

Galang-baru

Durian

Bang Basar

Pompong

Bengku

Temiang

Route of Operation Jaywick

Singapore

Dropoff area

Waiting area

Thursday Island

Cairns

Townsville

Exmouth

Brisbane

Sydney

SCALE

0   10   20 miles

0   10   20   30 kilometres

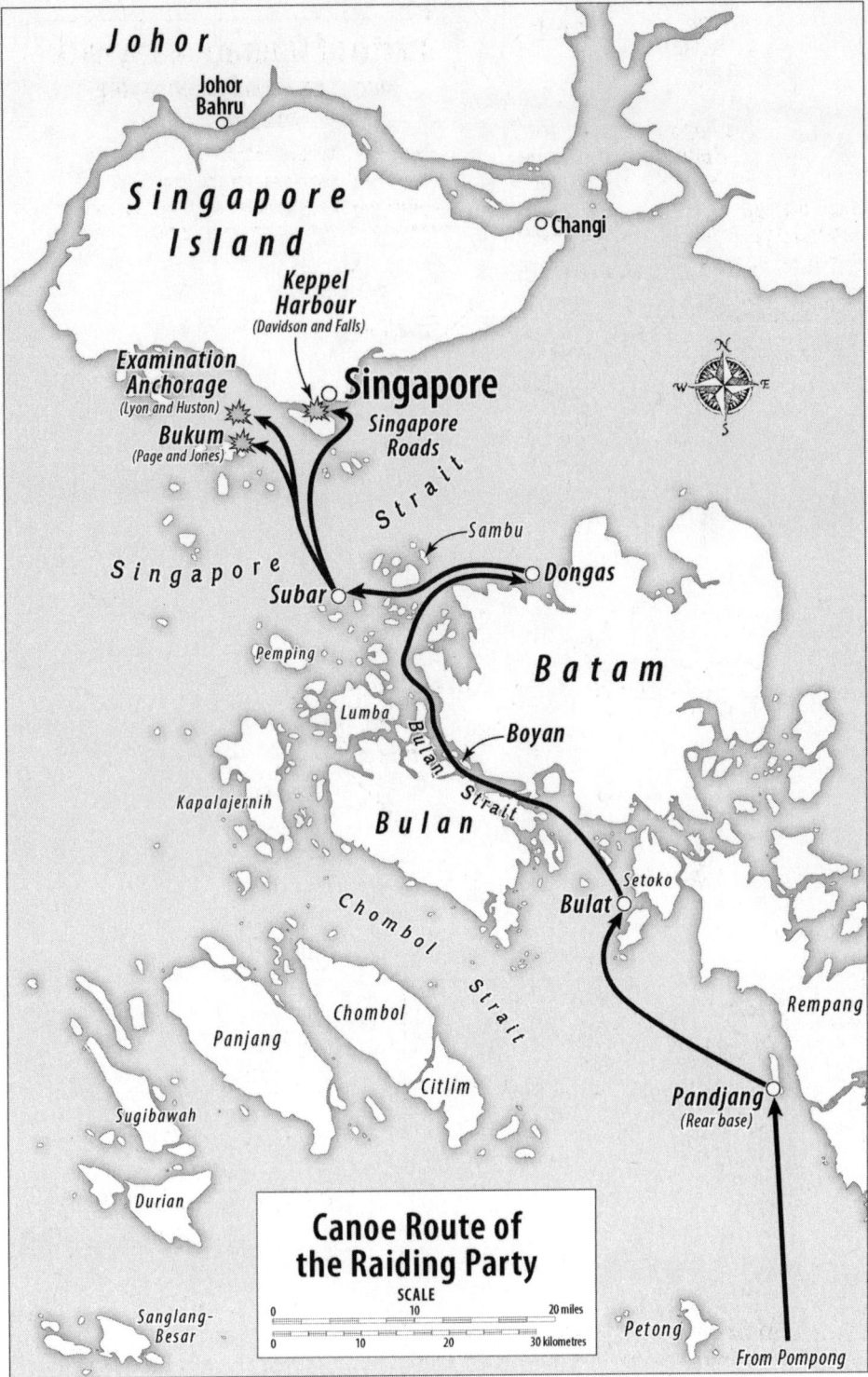

Johor

Johor Bahru

Singapore Island

Changi

Keppel Harbour
(Davidson and Falls)

Examination Anchorage
(Lyon and Huston)

Bukum
(Page and Jones)

Singapore

Singapore Roads

Singapore

Strait

Sambu

Subar

Dongas

Pemping

Batam

Lumba

Boyan

Bulan Strait

Kapalajernih

Bulan

Setoko

Bulat

Chombol Strait

Rempang

Panjang

Chombol

Citlim

Pandjang
(Rear base)

Sugibawah

Durian

Canoe Route of the Raiding Party

SCALE

0		10		20 miles

0	10	20	30 kilometres

Sanglang-Besar

Petong

From Pompong

Preface

It was a warm summer's day in 1969 when I first heard the remarkable story of a small wooden Japanese-built fishing vessel called the *Krait* and her role in one of the most audacious commando missions undertaken during World War II.

The late Australian war correspondent and author Ronald McKie, a friend of my father, Colin, gave me the job of mowing his large lawn on the side of Mount Gibraltar in my hometown of Bowral in the New South Wales Southern Highlands. When the mowing was done, he would treat me to a glass of lemonade in the cool of his study, whose walls were adorned with a collection of framed front pages showing his reports from the Asian and European theatres of World War II. McKie would also regale me with his adventures as a war correspondent, which to the eager ears of a 12-year-old boy were simply enthralling. They remain enthralling to this day.

One of the most extraordinary tales, which he had turned into a bestselling book, *The Heroes*, published in 1960, was the story of Operation Jaywick. This was the codename for a successful attack against Japanese shipping in Singapore harbour on the night of 26 September 1943. A second, but disastrous, mission a year later was codenamed Operation Rimau.

The Jaywick raid is the stuff of legend among special forces. But outside those specialised circles, it is well known only to Australians of the surviving wartime and immediate postwar generations, and military aficionados.

Still less familiar is the story of the small, nondescript timber fishing boat that carried the 14 Allied commandos into the heart of enemy territory and delivered them safely back home.

That story continues to this day as the boat undergoes a new, careful renovation at the hands of expert shipwrights to bring her back to her 1943 configuration and to claim her rightful position as the symbolic flagship of Australian special forces operations.

September 2018 marks the seventy-fifth anniversary of the *Krait*'s amazing journey, but there is much more to the story of 'the little boat that could'.

Ian McPhedran
Sydney 2018

Prologue

Late on the night of 26 September 1943, six young men with blackened faces paddling three canvas-covered, two-man folding canoes, slid silently into Singapore harbour at the sharp end of one of the most daring and successful special forces raids in the history of warfare.

As the lights of the occupied city blazed defiantly, none of the thousands of Japanese troops in the garrison, nor the hundreds of sailors on board the dozens of ships anchored in the harbour, could have imagined the cunning act of sabotage that was about to unfold.

Singapore in late 1943 was the impregnable heart of the rapidly expanding Japanese empire and a prison island for thousands of Australian and other Allied troops at the infamous Changi prisoner-of-war camp. Just like the British imperialists before him, the then Prime Minister of Japan, General Hideki Tojo, regarded the Japanese-occupied island as 'untouchable'.

After attaching magnetic limpet mines to seven ships, the six raiders sneaked out of the harbour at the start of an arduous and exhausting 80-kilometre island-hopping return paddle, hoping and praying that they would be able to rendezvous with their mother ship, the MV *Krait*, for the long voyage home to Australia.

Reaching their first lying-up position on a tiny island off Singapore several hours later, four of the saboteurs climbed a hill from where they could see the brilliant lights. They watched and listened in awe as seven Japanese vessels either went to the bottom of the harbour or sustained serious damage from the mines they had attached below the waterline.

Mostyn 'Moss' Berryman was a reserve canoeist who, instead of going on the raid, remained on board the *Krait* with seven shipmates while the vessel prowled around the islands and inlets of southern Borneo, hiding in plain sight disguised as a Japanese fishing boat and waiting to pick up the returning operatives.

Aged 95 and in 2018 the last survivor of Operation Jaywick, Berryman remembered the first time he laid eyes on the *Krait* as if it were yesterday.

The young navy volunteer and his mates had spent several weeks in training at the secret commando bush camp, known as Camp X, at Refuge Bay on the lower Hawkesbury River north of Sydney when, early one morning, a strange vessel motored into the bay. Berryman was taken aback by the sight of the ugly, squat, 21-metre timber boat. The keen 18-year-old sailor had expected to be posted to a nice big warship.

Seventy-five years later, at home in a retirement village in Adelaide, the clear-eyed, smartly dressed old gentleman recalled his commanding officer Captain Ivan Lyon ordering the team to paddle out and take a good look at the boat that would be their home for the next few months.

'It looked Japanese, it was named Japanese and it smelled Japanese. It was a bit fishy,' Berryman said. 'We climbed aboard and there was nothing there. She was as bare as a baby's behind; no fridge, no bunks, no toilet, no nothing.'

The men continued training hard and soon became experts at assembling special canvas-covered two-man folding canoes, or 'folboats', in double-quick time and paddling them over long distances in a variety of sea states. Around the camp fire at night they would speculate about what their top-secret mission could be and where this rickety-looking boat could possibly carry them. After some argy bargy the consensus was that the enemy-held port city of Rabaul on the island of New Britain in New Guinea was the most likely target.

'We had read that there was a big harbour there, and there was going to be something to be blown up in Rabaul,' Berryman recalled.

Not one of the young operatives imagined that the real target for their 'strange' boat and her highly trained crew would be the enemy fortress of Singapore.

'As it turned out, we broke the world record,' Berryman said with justifiable pride. 'Nobody in the history of the world had ever gone that far into enemy territory and come out alive.'

A VERY
SPECIAL
BUNCH

1

A twist of fate

Millions of visitors to the Australian National Maritime Museum in Sydney's Darling Harbour have strolled past the array of historic vessels on display in the water, but few might have noticed, let alone paid much attention to a black, low-slung, wooden ex-fishing vessel that was moored behind a locked gate for years.

Far more impressive to the casual eye are the old Oberon-class submarine HMAS *Onslow*, the destroyer HMAS *Vampire* and the beautiful replica of Captain Cook's ship HMB *Endeavour* that grace the waters outside the museum.

Yet it was this very ability to avoid attention that enabled the modest former Japanese fishing boat, the MV *Krait*, to travel further behind enemy lines than any other vessel in history and then sink more enemy shipping than any Australian warship during World War II.

Only a global conflict could throw up such a bizarre twist of fate that would see a boat built in Japan in 1934 – seven years before that country even entered the war – morph into one of Australia's most important monuments to human imagination and courage.

Over the years, many tourists strolling by on Remembrance Day, 11 November, gave no more than a passing glance, if that, to an old man as he bent down at exactly 11 am to lay a flower in the water next to the little boat. This was a pilgrimage that the late World War II 'Z' Special Unit veteran Douglas Herps made for years from his home in the genteel suburb of Woollahra.

It was his way of honouring not only the 14 men who served in MV *Krait*, but all those from the top-secret special operations units, including his own 'Z' Special Unit, who paid the ultimate sacrifice during clandestine missions throughout Southeast Asia and New Guinea during World War II. Some were his mates; many others he had never met and would never meet, such was the secretive cell-like operating structure of the units that were the predecessors of the modern-day Special Air Service and Commando regiments.

'Z' Special Unit was established to administer the army and civilian members who operated under the umbrella of Special Operations Australia. Like many former wartime special forces operatives, Herps took his legal responsibilities for keeping official secrets very seriously and even 70 years after the war had ended he was reluctant to discuss his own role in any detail. He would take those secrets to the grave, as he had solemnly sworn to do. However, he was happy to talk at great length and with passion about the sacrifice of the many operatives who did not come home.

One of his earlier projects had been to document and photograph the graves of fallen 'Z' members in war cemeteries from Singapore to St Louis in the US. To him, the faces of these brave young men – and they were very young – were still fresh and the *Krait* was a tangible reminder of the audacity, stealth and sheer balls of the hundreds of men who paddled, swam, marched or parachuted behind enemy lines to conduct the sort of clandestine missions of which legends might be made, if only people knew of them.

Many veterans and serving special forces troops regard the *Krait* as a floating war memorial. They believe that the boat is as solemn and important an icon as any 'official' monument in the land.

As he made his annual pilgrimages down to the harbour, Herps became increasingly worried about the condition of the vessel while she lay in the water, year after year, beside the museum. That concern became a passion and then an obsession as the old soldier, who knew that his time on this earth was limited, became one of the prime movers behind a push to restore and ensure the preservation of the MV *Krait* for all time.

He made it his personal mission and left no stone unturned. A successful businessman since the war, he tapped every influential contact he had ever made (and a lot he hadn't) to drive the project.

In his quest to preserve the *Krait* and the memory of his fallen 'Z' Special Unit colleagues, Herps was a master at bringing outsiders on board. From politicians to business people and professors to plumbers, once he went to work on someone they were soon supporting the cause – or begging for mercy.

He soon enlisted me in his campaign. We had met previously when he had called me out of the blue to discuss an article I had written about 'Z' Special. He later agreed to be interviewed for one of my books, *Too Bold to Die*, which included a section of interviews with other surviving former 'Z' Special operatives and examined the nature of valour. When he discovered that I had a childhood connection with Ronald McKie, author of *The Heroes*, he knew he had me hooked.

Using his network, he also got in touch with prominent media figures such as 2GB shock jock Alan Jones and Sky TV's Graham Richardson, the former Labor politician turned commentator. Herps also successfully lobbied the ABC to make an episode of the popular series *Australian Story* about the *Krait* and his mission to save her. This screened in 2015 and again in 2017, helping to bring the story of the *Krait* and Operation Jaywick to a new audience.

Herps summed up his feelings for the small boat during an interview for the *Australian Story* program. 'When I personally look at it, I see mates of mine who were killed. We regard it as a war memorial, and that's what we want it to be.'

The director of the Australian War Memorial, former Defence Minister Dr Brendan Nelson, needed no convincing about the importance of the vessel. He regards the *Krait*, owned by the memorial but on long-term loan to the ANMM, as one of the most significant objects in the war memorial's 4 million-strong collection, after the bullet-riddled Ascot Gallipoli landing boat and the World War II Lancaster bomber, *G for George*.

Renewed concerns over the future of the vessel had been mounting for some time as she became increasingly unseaworthy. Both institutions knew they would need much deeper pockets to keep her afloat for many more years, let alone restore her to her historic 1943 configuration and exhibit her properly.

In 2015 the ANMM drew up a draft vessel management plan for the *Krait*, followed by the final version in 2016. According to the report, the *Krait* began life in Nagahama Port on the island of Shikoku as the *Kohfuku Maru*, which translates as 'Good

Fortune' or 'Happiness'. She plied her trade as a fish carrier and supply vessel, supporting the fishing fleet that worked the waters around the Anambas Islands in the South China Sea, northeast of Singapore.

She was designed along the lines of English steam-powered seine or driftnet fishing boats and the 68-tonne, 21-metre by 3.5-metre vessel's flexibility allowed her to be easily transformed into a freighter or even a passenger boat. However, the lack of facilities such as a toilet, bunks or even seats, let alone a galley, meant that anyone unfortunate enough to find themselves on board as a passenger would be really roughing it.

One thing in the boat's favour was her extremely solid teak and Muntz metal (an alloy of 60 per cent copper and 40 per cent zinc) sheathing construction that kept her seaworthy for decades and, despite her narrow beam, low freeboard and rolling gait, allowed her to operate safely in a variety of sea states.

Official records show that *Kohfuku Maru* was at the dock in Singapore on 7 December 1941 when Japan launched its devastating surprise Pacific offensive against Pearl Harbor, Thailand, the Philippines and Malaya (now Malaysia). Her two sister ships, *Fukuyu Maru 2163* and *Shofuku Maru 2205*, were out at sea on that fateful day and were impounded and later destroyed by the Royal Australian Navy.

A 60-year-old Australian master mariner Bill Reynolds from Williamstown in Victoria, spotted *Kohfuku Maru* lying at the wharf. Reynolds had been working throughout Southeast Asia in the lead-up to World War II. Earlier, he had joined the Perak Local Defence Corps in Malaya and had been involved in blowing up anything that might be of use to the invading Japanese.

Reynolds, a World War I Royal Navy veteran, merchant seaman, mining engineer and old Singapore hand, recruited a

13

team of Chinese workers to help refurbish the vessel and make her seaworthy.

The *Kohfuku Maru* was constructed using 45-centimetre frame spacings with a 2.3-metre bar keel and a loaded draught of 1.5-metres forward and 2.2-metres aft. She had a top speed of about 8.5 knots (15.7 kilometres) per hour and a range of 8000 nautical miles (14,800 kilometres). She was powered by a Deutz four-cylinder diesel engine located below the 2-centimetre-thick teak deck and astern of the 2-metre-square wheelhouse located astern of amidships.

Forward of the wheelhouse were four cork-lined cargo holds and a fold-down mast. Astern of the wheelhouse, a canvas awning covered the rear deck to the stern of the vessel. It also had canvas curtains that could be lowered to the bulwarks.

The 'head', or toilet, consisted of a bucket on a rope fixed to the stern and nearby was a primitive petrol stove and small oven. Protruding through the awning were the engine's exhaust and ventilation pipes. The only built-in sleeping facility on board was a single bunk in the wheelhouse that doubled as a seat for the helmsman. Above that was a fold-down chart table.

In February 1942, just days before the demise of the British fortress, Reynolds steered the now seaworthy *Kohfuku Maru* away from the wharf in Singapore. Through a combination of good judgment and even better luck he managed to evade the advancing Japanese forces.

Reynolds decided to head east through the Riouw Strait to Bintan Island rather than south with the rest of the vessels that were fleeing the invaders. He was thus able to evade capture and then rescue, in just two weeks, more than 1500 desperate souls who were trying to escape from Singapore towards the Dutch East Indies.

During the chaos of the invasion and the evacuation of Singapore, Reynolds had encountered 27-year-old British Army Captain Ivan Lyon of the Gordon Highlander Regiment and his Welsh batman, Corporal Ron 'Taffy' Morris. Lyon and Morris were also rescuing refugees. All three men were heading for the port of Rengat, some 60 kilometres up the Indragiri River on the Indonesian island of Sumatra. The town was one of the main staging points for evacuees from Singapore.

According to Ronald McKie's book *The Heroes*, Lyon's boat almost collided with the *Kohfuku Maru* at the town's wharf and Reynolds let fly with a tirade of abuse that led to a few drinks of forgiveness, the birth of a strong friendship – and a daring idea.

Putting their heads together, Reynolds and Lyon soon realised that since the unassuming craft had escaped from Singapore right under the noses of the enemy, there was no reason why she couldn't make the journey in reverse. And so the plan to attack Singapore, which they codenamed 'Jock Force', was born. It later morphed into Operation Jaywick, named after a seaside village in Essex, England where fishing boats similar in looks to *Kohfuku Maru* were commonplace.

The plan was fine with the daring Reynolds who, when he was in the merchant marine, had travelled to Islam's holy site of Mecca in 1925, disguised as a Muslim pilgrim. The equally game Lyon was an agent with Britain's MI6 foreign intelligence service and the top-secret military intelligence unit Special Operations Executive (SOE), based in Singapore. He too knew the region like the back of his hand.

Reynolds, who had spent years plying the waters around Singapore and Malaya, eventually sailed *Kohfuku Maru* – under a Chinese flag and bearing the assumed Chinese name of *Suey Sin Fah* (meaning star-shaped flower) – with a cargo of refugees on an epic voyage from Sumatra via the Malacca Strait to Ceylon (now Sri Lanka) and on to Bombay (now Mumbai) in India.

Lyon and Morris also sailed from Sumatra to Ceylon under even harsher conditions in an old sailing proa (twin-hulled vessel) called the *Sederhana Johannes*.

It was thus in Ceylon that Reynolds was reunited with Captain Lyon and the pair went to work on their daring plan. Fortunately, the commander-in-chief of British forces in India and the Far East, General Archibald Wavell, who was a strong supporter of unconventional warfare, took little convincing of the merits of their audacious plot to strike at the heart of the enemy. Lyon had used his extensive list of contacts to arrange a meeting with Wavell at his headquarters in New Delhi. However, he insisted that if it proceeded, the operation was to be mounted from Australia and that any attack should come from the east of Singapore, rather than from the west as Reynolds and Lyon had initially proposed. Wavell argued that the waters to the west of the island were dominated by the Japanese who, he said, would not expect an attack from the east.

Because of engine trouble and the inevitable wartime delays, the plan for Reynolds to sail the boat – to be renamed *Krait* after a highly venomous Indian snake – to Australia was scuttled. She was eventually shipped as deck cargo on board a freighter to Sydney Harbour, where Bill Reynolds rejoined the vessel, by then under the management of the Royal Navy.

In July 1942, Ivan Lyon arrived at the Melbourne headquarters of the Allied Intelligence Bureau's Inter-Allied Services Department, a sub-unit of SOE and the forerunner of Special Operations Australia. At that time it was housed in 'Airlie', at 260 Domain Road, South Yarra.

The outlandish plan was already well advanced in Lyon's

mind. The operation would be a British run and funded show, conducted jointly by SOE and the RAN. The plan was strongly supported by the RAN's head of Naval Intelligence Commander Rupert 'Cocky' Long.

Despite much postwar confusion and many claims to the contrary, 'Z' Special Unit was established in June 1942 for the administration of the army and civilian members of the ISD and to support the conduct of special operations. In mid-1942, control of the AIB passed to the Supreme Commander, Southwest Pacific Area, US General Douglas MacArthur, whose objectives were spelled out in plain English in a general headquarters directive on 6 July:

> The mission of Allied Intelligence Bureau will be to obtain and report information of the enemy in the Southwest Pacific Area … and in addition, where practicable, to weaken the enemy by sabotage and destruction of morale and to lend aid and assistance to local efforts to the same end in enemy occupied territories.

That was a clear articulation of the role of SOA and the 'Z' Special Unit. Australia, the Netherlands and the United States funded the bureau to the tune of £60,000 each. Its area of operations was vast, stretching from the China coast in the north to Timor in the south, and from Thailand in the west to New Guinea in the east.

By July 1942 'Z' Special Unit had inserted operatives into Timor, Java and New Guinea. It had also established the top-secret training camp called 'Z' Experimental Station (ZES) at a property known only as the 'house on the hill' on the outskirts of Cairns.

In September 1943, after the *Krait* and her crew departed for Singapore on the top-secret Operation Jaywick, the Cairns house was closed and 'Z' Special Unit training was shifted to Fraser Island in the south.

Despite major misgivings among some top brass, Lyon found two willing allies for his outrageous plan in the director of AIB, Colonel Caleb Roberts, and the head of ISD, Lieutenant Colonel Egerton Mott. Then, by a stroke of sheer luck, soon after he arrived from India Lyon was reunited at a social event in Melbourne with another tough and able former Singapore hand, the naval Lieutenant Donald Davidson, who would become his second-in-command.

Lyon, the son of a general officer and graduate of the Royal Military Academy Sandhurst, ran his operation from a top-secret location in Potts Point, Sydney, with funds flowing directly from SOE in London to an account at the Bank of New South Wales branch in nearby Kings Cross. The first instalment was £30,000, a small fortune at a time when Sydney's average house price was about £600.

The funds and the administration of the plan was managed by Major Jock Campbell of the King's Own Scottish Borderers, who had been a rubber grower in Malaya and had escaped to India with Lyon and Taffy Morris.

Lyon's motivation for the mission had received a jolt following his arrival in Australia, when he had learned that the enemy had imprisoned his wife, Gabrielle, and his baby son, Clive, in Japan after their ship, the SS *Nankin*, had been captured by the German raider *Thor*, en route from Fremantle to India in May. They were repatriated to Australia after the war.

Once the operation had cleared the final hurdles and been approved by the Australian commander-in-chief, General Sir

Thomas Blamey – with the help of a Lyon family friend and then Governor General of Australia, Lord Gowrie, VC – Lyon and Davidson set about selecting the team they would need for the top-secret 'Jock Force' and the audacious mission that would become Operation Jaywick.

2

Putting the band together

Donald Davidson was a tough–as–nails character who had worked as a jackaroo in outback Queensland and had developed a reputation as a powerful, fearless bloke.

When the war began, he was working in the teak forests of Burma and after he was denied permission to join the army he enlisted as a Lieutenant in the Royal Navy (RN). Following a narrow escape from Sandakan in Borneo, he was posted to the navy office in Melbourne in March 1942.

In a postwar interview with Brisbane documentary-maker John Schindler for his film *Tigers and Snakes*, the *Krait*'s radio operator, Horrie Young, described Davidson as a highly respected 'man's man' who earned his respect by deed rather than rank.

'He gained the respect of the men because he would do whatever they would do and he in most cases would do it better,' said Young. 'He would never ask anybody to do anything that he was not prepared to do himself and he was very capable, a very powerful man, too.'

He first met Davidson in July 1943 when he was in training for landing-barge beach signals duty at the navy's Combined Operations Training Centre HMAS *Assault* at Port Stephens in New South Wales. According to Young's war diary the training was tough, and as a signaller he would often be forced to wade ashore from a landing craft stuck on a sandbank through cold water up to his neck, weighed down by full webbing and heavy radio equipment.

Davidson and his team arrived at Port Stephens looking for a volunteer radio man.

'Their leader was a tall, fearsome-looking fellow whose steely eyes seemed to bore right through whoever happened to be speaking to him,' wrote Horrie Young in a mid-1990s memoir. 'I was shortly to learn that his name was Lieutenant Donald Davidson, RNR, and that he was indeed on special duties with an organisation bearing the unheard-of title, "Services Reconnaissance Department" [SRD formed in April 1943]. There was whispered speculation that this group was somehow connected with the Special Operations Executive, the highly secret group set up by the British prime minister after the fall of France whose prime objective was to cause as much disruption and discomfort to the enemy as possible.'

Davidson appeared to embody this self-same discomfort. 'He arrived supported by a small group of naval ratings similarly green-clothed in army attire who seemed to be continually "bashing" each other up in what to them was recreation, but in fact was unarmed combat training. Indeed, this group, during the course of their brief stay, was to treat us "beach commandos" to some spectacular performances of the martial arts including thrust and parry with some particularly wicked looking knives – quite realistic as I well recall.'

Young was only too pleased to put up his hand to join Davidson's intriguing team of operators. He soon found himself heading north to Cairns and the 'house on the hill'.

* * *

Just a week after their initial meeting in July, Lyon and Davidson were at the Flinders Naval Depot southeast of Melbourne, selecting volunteers. Some 40 keen young Australians put their hands up for unspecified 'special service' and 17 likely lads were selected for further training.

During six tough weeks at the Army Physical and Recreational Training School at Frankston on Port Phillip Bay, Davidson put them through their paces, watching closely for any weakness or character flaws as they boxed, wrestled, climbed, ran and learned unarmed combat.

Moss Berryman, one of those 17 young volunteers, had vivid memories of the initial training at what he called the 'commando school' and he described their unusual welcome to the Frankston facility.

'We were met by the major in charge of the camp and we were going to be shown around before dinner,' Berryman recalled. 'As we were marching around through some scrub, we were jumped on by a group of Americans who were there doing the same training as we were going to have. They rubbed our noses in the sand and that was our introduction into this commando school. It was a pretty tough sort of a school.'

The training was arduous and went on around the clock. Berryman remembered an exercise which involved running up and down sandhills until the new recruits thought their legs would drop off – yet they had to keep going.

'I've seen grown boys cry with pain after trips up and down those sandhills on the beach at Frankston. Daytime and night time didn't mean a thing. You could be sound asleep at two in the morning – "All up, all up, put your sandshoes on, we're going for a run".'

Finally, in early September 1942 six of the men were told that they hadn't made the grade and would return to their units. The remaining 11 were informed that they would be leaving Victoria on the Sydney express train, their ultimate destination a secret bush training camp on the Hawkesbury River north of the city.

Their first sight of the estuary was at Bobbin Head on the upper reaches of Cowan Creek. Surrounded by dense bushland and sandstone outcrops it was hard to believe that they were so close to the nation's biggest city. After a 15-kilometre motorboat ride downstream past Cottage Point towards Broken Bay they turned right into Refuge Bay, a scenic little inlet at the junction of Cowan Creek and the Hawkesbury River, about 6 kilometres from Pittwater and the sea. The area's numerous inlets, bays and cliffs and its proximity to Pittwater and across Broken Bay to the Brisbane Water, Pearl Beach and Patonga and on to Gosford made it the ideal training ground for the planned Jaywick raid.

They came ashore on a small sandy beach littered with tents, food and cooking supplies, and the first order of business was to carry their new homes up to the top of the sandstone cliff guarding the bay, where they were to establish their secret training base.

'That was an exercise in itself, taking all that stuff up the cliff,' Berryman recalled. 'We got it up there and somehow or other we got the tents up, made up our beds and we got a feed – and that was our introduction to the Hawkesbury River.'

Davidson implemented a strict daily training regime that began at first light and ended at 10 pm, with many late-night exercises thrown in for good measure. The focus was on canoeing, fitness, hand-to-hand combat, night navigation, and weapons and explosives.

The men cleared an area around the tents for a training ground and when they weren't on the water or running marathons they would wrestle and practise unarmed combat and learn the dark arts of killing a man with bare hands, a cord, knife, jungle parang (machete) or blackjack baton.

They were taught how to navigate on land and water by day and night, how to read maps and charts, how to camouflage themselves and their equipment, climb cliffs and go without food and water for long periods.

Davidson's diary, held by the Australian National Archives in Canberra, includes the finer details of how best to kill or maim an enemy fighter with your bare hands.

First, the vulnerable points of the body: 'Temple, good hard blow will kill. Eyes, gouge out in fighting, jab with two fingers in sudden movement, finish off at leisure … Ears, pull off, bite off, exert pressure upwards with both thumbs under bottoms of ears … Adam's apple, punch as Japanese do with second or long finger knuckled and protruding … Hands, tear fingers apart and split hands, bend fingers back and break,' Davidson wrote matter-of-factly.

Then came unarmed combat and the numerous methods of attacking and countering enemy moves. This included the handy skill of 'stalking and carrying off sentry and tying to tree' as well as 'reaching through crutch from the rear seizing clothing, jerking opponent off feet and crushing testicles and throwing'.

Two army instructors turned up one day and began teaching the men how to use and maintain a variety of unusual weapons, including the Sten, Owen and Lewis guns and the heavier Bren machine gun, as well as explosives. But the main focus was always on physical fitness. Both Lyon and Davidson were the type of officers who would never ask their men to do anything that they would not do themselves.

Moss Berryman recalled being woken several times at two in the morning and going for a 35-kilometre run around to Palm Beach. 'We'd run through the scrub for a few miles until we hit a bit of a dirt road and we'd run a few miles down this dirt road, then we'd walk and run a few miles on the highway coming back around to the entrance where the Hawkesbury entered the sea. After a brief rest, they would conduct beach sports.'

One day, a pair of two-man folding canvas canoes arrived at the camp. Several versions of the folboats had been tested secretly throughout Australia with a view to employing them on both the Jaywick raid and a second raid on Rabaul that was codenamed Scorpion. The craft were based on German, Swiss and British designs that had been improved since their invention in the 1920s.

Eventually, more than 1000 of the canoes were manufactured in Australia during the war by the Swiss immigrant and folboat designer Walter Hoehn. Their first known operational deployment was in New Ireland in New Guinea in July 1942. The last operation using the craft was Operation Semut 4 in Sarawak in August 1945. Hoehn provided the first two canoes that were used by the Jaywick team at Refuge Bay.

As soon as the folboats arrived, the group of potential operatives started training in the surf at Palm Beach to get used to paddling them in rough water, Berryman recalled. And no sooner had they finished their first session than Captain Lyon announced that they would be running the 35 kilometres back to camp. They arrived late at night and thoroughly exhausted.

The two folboats gradually became the main focus of the training and as each day passed the distances became greater until one day Lyon and three men, including Berryman, took off for a four-day paddle up the coast to Newcastle, about 90 kilometres 'as the crow flies'. It wasn't a straightforward exercise, however, as they travelled much of the way via the waterways that link Tuggerah Lake, about 48 kilometres south of Newcastle, with Lake Macquarie, about 13 kilometres southwest of Newcastle. That meant carrying the canoes several kilometres overland between the lakes.

'At night-time, we used to sleep on the veranda of the local school then get up very early in the morning, have a bit of a wash and a drink of water and away we'd go before the kids started to arrive at school. So nobody virtually saw us,' Berryman recalled.

As the men became expert at handling the canoes, Lyon and Davidson observed them very closely, making a note of who was short-tempered or sulky; who argued or complained. Lyon's diary includes ample evidence of his tough approach to selection. He described one of the 11 potential operatives as 'rather lazy, gutless, no stability, mentally childish. Would not rely on him even in small things.'

Another, who was left in the camp with Davidson during Christmas leave, was described as 'lazy and surly. One cannot like the man however hard one tries.'

Yet another was regarded as a 'bumptious little guttersnipe and will always be a serious irritant to those around him. Informed him that he was to go. Took him into Balmoral [Naval Depot] for disposal.'

Moss Berryman needn't have worried about Davidson's view of him. In the diary, Davidson described the young sailor as 'very quiet and subdued, you never notice he is in camp. Not a leader yet but of the type that would make a good officer with age and experience. Needs a bit more push.'

After about three months at the camp Captain Lyon called the men together and announced that the final five for the mission had been chosen and the remaining six would be immediately leaving for Balmoral Naval Depot to await further orders.

The non-commissioned members of Jock Force ranged in age from 18 to 23. They were Acting Able Seaman Moss Berryman, a shop assistant from Adelaide; Walter 'Poppa' Falls, a dairy farmer from Casino, New South Wales (the oldest at 23, hence his nickname); Andrew 'Happy' Huston from Brisbane, who seldom smiled; Fred 'Boof' Marsh, also from Brisbane, who was a practical joker and expert in unarmed combat; and the only man with sea time in the navy, Arthur 'Joe' Jones from Perth.

They would be joined by Taffy Morris for the first leg of their long journey aboard *Krait*, with Captain Reynolds and Lieutenant Davidson making up the eight. Lyon would join her in Cairns and other crew would be added along the way.

The vessel departed from Refuge Bay on 18 January 1943 and as she limped and rolled north up the coast with her unreliable Deutz engine regularly giving up the ghost, she was forced to call in at Brisbane for urgent repairs. There, a veteran Irish engineer, Paddy McDowell, and an experienced navy sailor, Leading Seaman Kevin 'Cobber' Cain, joined the crew.

After yet another breakdown, in the Whitsunday Islands, the *Krait* had to be towed into Townsville. Here, Bill Reynolds left the mission. According to Australian War Memorial documents, his new masters in American intelligence diverted him to other duties before the *Krait* was able to depart from Cairns on her operation, so he missed out on seeing the plan come to fruition with Lyon.

The rest of Reynolds' story is tragic. The mission on which he was sent — cruising through the occupied islands to Australia's north posing as a trader — went awry. He was given up by local villagers and captured by the Japanese in November 1943.

In February 1944, Reynolds was transferred from Balikpapan in eastern Borneo to Surabaya in Java. He was held there in solitary confinement for six months before being executed by firing squad on 8 August 1944. His body was buried in an unmarked grave.

Before his execution he managed to scratch the grim details of his capture and brutal treatment at the hands of his Japanese captors into the doorframe of his cell. This vital piece of the William Roy Reynolds story was ultimately used in evidence in war crimes trials and was donated to the Australian War Memorial in 1946.

From Townsville the little boat carried on to Cairns and camp ZES, where they were joined by four more members of the team — Captain Lyon; Army Lieutenant and medical student Bob Page; Acting Leading Telegraphist Horrie Young; and the new skipper and navigator, Naval Reserve Lieutenant Ted Carse.

Page had been a member of the team codenamed Scorpion that had been training for a raid on Rabaul that was later cancelled, and he was paddling one of the five two-man folboats that successfully 'attacked' the heavily guarded Townsville harbour during a training mission in June 1942. This 'raid' proved to the powers-that-be that an attack by canoe could work even in a well-guarded navy port.

Following the successful Townsville dress rehearsal Page was transferred to Ivan Lyon's Jock Force. At that point, the crew was all but complete except for the vital position of ship's cook, so Lyon drove up to the Wongabel military transit camp near Atherton, inland from Cairns, to find the final member of the team.

Andy Crilly was an army engineer who had been fighting with the 24th Field Company in New Guinea when he was wounded during the Milne Bay campaign in December 1942. A corporal, he was at Wongabel awaiting reassignment in August 1943 when a parade was called for an address from a rather odd British major.

In an account of his wartime experiences written by Crilly that is held by his youngest son, former Army Warrant Officer and Commando Tony Crilly in Albury, New South Wales, he said that Lyon called for one volunteer and said 'very definitely that the mission was so dangerous … that he stated openly that the party might not come back'.

After the married and attached men were weeded out, one of the seven remaining men asked Lyon where the job was and whether there would be any fighting. He just laughed. That left six men standing and the Scottish-born Crilly was finally chosen to fill the final berth on the *Krait* as the boat's cook.

'I'm not much of a cook, but I'm a pretty good motor mechanic,' he told the officer.

That was how 'Pancake Andy', as his shipmates would christen him, became the fourteenth and last man to join Operation Jaywick. His culinary skills were limited to pancakes, hence the nickname. Indeed, none of the Jaywick men who survived the war ever wanted to see another pancake.

The next day a car arrived at Wongabel at 5 am to transfer Crilly to Cairns and the 'house on the hill'.

'There was one British corporal and eight sailors and they were a top class lot of men,' he wrote. 'The motto was "eat well for you will be hungry for a long time". The cook was fit for a hotel and he turned out some very good meals.'

The luxury didn't last, however, and when army engineer Crilly was asked if he was happy to live like a sailor and 'eat from a tin and keep fit by playing cards and wrestling on the engine room hatch', he replied, 'Without the army, the navy is lost.'

As is so often the case, Andy Crilly did not escape the war mentally unscathed. His three older children, Ann, Carmel and Andrew, remember spending many Sundays of their childhoods visiting him at the Greenslopes Repatriation General Hospital in Brisbane.

The children were 11, eight and five respectively when Andy died, and they knew nothing about his war service until years later when a reporter turned up at their house in 1963 to write about their father, the war hero. The two youngest children, Margaret and Tony, were just three and 14 months. Even his wife, Patricia, who died in November 2010, had had no inkling about Crilly's war service, including Operation Jaywick.

'Greenslopes was a big outing for us every Sunday,' Ann recalled. 'More often than not he was in hospital. For the entire time mum was carrying Tony, he was in hospital. We knew nothing at all about the war but I do remember quite a few times going to Brisbane to visit Ted Carse and his wife. We were never able to talk to him [Andy] about what had happened.'

Young Andrew's only hint of his dad's past was a commando's leather cosh, or truncheon, that he played with. Crilly also held onto his revolver, which was kept in a bathroom cabinet (minus its firing pin).

'He would never talk about the army, or war, or any of the atrocities he saw, with us,' Andrew said.

Carmel is sure that her dad had undiagnosed post-traumatic stress disorder resulting from his war service.

'It didn't matter what time of the night I got up to go to the bathroom or how late I went to bed, he was always sitting in his chair. I don't think he ever slept,' she said.

Andy Crilly was passionately anti-war and his daughters recalled that whenever reports came onto the wireless about the Vietnam War he would immediately get up and switch it off. The children have no memory of 'Pancake Andy' ever cooking pancakes, but they say he was a wizard at doughnuts, porridge and plum pudding or the Scottish specialty Cootie dumpling. He even constructed a special doughnut maker, to the delight of his kids.

'He'd make the batter, put the fat in the pot and then he would lower the batter into the pot ... he definitely made that special thing to make doughnuts,' Ann said.

'He was born in Scotland and he was very proud of his children and he wanted the best for us,' said Carmel.

She added that her father was not even close to the ocker Australian as portrayed by actor Gerry Skilton in the 1989 British–Australian TV miniseries about Jaywick. Called *The Heroes* and based on the Jaywick part of McKie's book – which describes Crilly simply as 'a Queenslander' – the production was a huge success, especially in Britain. The scriptwriter was the successful Australian screenwriter, playwright and novelist Peter Yeldham.

Carmel also recalled that she was offered two jobs, one in Perth and one in Brisbane, as a direct result of being Andy's daughter. In both cases the interviewer knew about her father's service and asked if she was his daughter.

'I got the jobs purely and simply because of who I was!'

Andy Crilly may not have told his children anything about his war but plenty of other veterans have, along with his written account, filled in the gaps. As an army veteran himself, Tony Crilly holds his dad's original medals, including his Military Medal (MM), and the other children all have copies.

3

The 'Admiral'

It was 12 January 1943 when naval reservist Sub Lieutenant Ted Carse knocked on the gate of 'Airlie' in South Yarra. He was carrying a letter of introduction from his old mate and head of Naval Intelligence, 'Cocky' Long. This would prove to be Carse's first taste of the shadowy world of special operations.

In researching *The Heroes*, McKie worked closely with Carse, who helped him reconstruct the details of Operation Jaywick from both his memory and his diaries.

Once inside the stately Victorian mansion, Carse told McKie, he was introduced to a Colonel Egerton Mott, who asked him whether he knew the islands to Australia's north and whether he could navigate.

'Have you any guts?' the gruff officer barked.

Carse chose not to answer the leading question and stood

silently waiting for the next instalment of what was obviously a character assessment.

'We're running a dangerous organisation and we want a navigator. That's why I asked to see you. If you were selected to the job could you take a ship from Melbourne to San Francisco?'

'I could take her anywhere,' Carse replied.

The colonel relaxed and smiled. 'I like you. Would you care to join our organisation?'

Carse almost laughed out loud, but he said, 'That depends. I don't know what it is or anything about it.'

Mott replied that it could involve operations behind enemy lines and that it could be most dangerous. 'But until you join us I can't tell you more – and not much even then.'

So Carse agreed to join. Mott then instructed him to proceed to the 'house on the hill' in Cairns, using an army movement order. His unit number would be 119.

'I must impress upon you the need for the utmost security. Your life is unimportant – quite unimportant – but the security of the organisation is vital,' Colonel Mott told him.

As he drank a couple of badly needed beers at the Botanical Hotel nearby in South Yarra and pondered what had been the most bizarre 30 minutes of his life, Carse didn't give a second thought to the two men talking horseracing at the bar. It would be some time before he found out that the 'spooks' had not only followed him all afternoon but were also on hand at Spencer Street railway station that night to make sure he caught the Sydney express.

Hubert Edward Carse was born at Rutherglen in northern Victoria and graduated from the Naval College at Jervis Bay in late 1918 after joining as a 13-year-old cadet.

Aged 21, he left the navy at the rank of an acting sub lieutenant and became a schoolteacher, but that landlocked career lasted barely two years before wanderlust took hold and he sailed the world as an able seaman in a British merchant ship. A stint as third mate in a Norwegian tramp steamer was followed by the purchase of a lugger at Thursday Island and time spent fishing for pearl shell and sea slug out of Darwin.

Upon the outbreak of war in 1939 and after various jobs including cleaner, camel driver and SP bookie, the hard-drinking Carse tried to join up but was deemed unfit due to bronchial trouble. It would be three long years and in the darkest days of the war in 1942 by the time the navy relented and, on 9 September 1942, made the Royal Australian Navy Volunteer Reservist a sub lieutenant based at HMAS *Magnetic* in Townsville. He was promoted to the rank of lieutenant on 4 January 1943.

Carse's service record, dated 28 February 1943 – just six weeks after that fateful meeting with Mott – is held in the National Archives of Australia. It describes him as an 'average officer who is reliable and trustworthy'.

'Unfortunately, his appearance is against him. Is loyal and respectful and works hard,' the document notes drily.

A later assessment dated 9 November 1944 describes him as 'An average officer who has been exemplary in the discharge of his duties. A pleasant if somewhat rugged personality with a strongly developed sense of humour. Is popular with his shipmates.'

The least flattering report, about his service at HMAS *Magnetic* and dated 12 August 1945, says: 'His work has been fair. His reliability generally is not more than average.'

Later that year on 3 December, however, his record of service at HMAS *Kuttabul* states that he was 'a zealous and conscientious officer who carries out his duties in a satisfactory manner'.

It was in Townsville that Carse had met Cocky Long, who suggested that he might have something more interesting for him to be doing than messing around with old boats and getting drunk on rest days.

Carse's drinking would come in for considerable attention and criticism in some books about the Singapore raid, but all his confidential service records include a question that asks if he was 'of temperate habit'. In all cases the answer is 'yes' and, in all cases, his general conduct is marked 'satisfactory'.

In his 2010 interview with John Schindler, Jaywick radio operator Horrie Young, from Perth, was at great pains to defend his skipper's reputation on the record.

'Well, there were criticisms that Ted used to drink a bit but show me the sailor that doesn't drink,' said Young. 'That's about all he's got. When his ship comes in, is to go ashore and find the nearest hotel and drown his sorrows. In other words, get a good clean drink of grog. So, he's no different to any other sailor.'

He added firmly that he had never seen Carse or anyone else drink aboard the *Krait* except for one brief celebratory toast.

So it was that several weeks after his meeting with Long, the 42-year-old Carse was in Melbourne, agreeing to join an organisation that regarded his life as 'unimportant'. A week after that he was a priority passenger on a military flight from Sydney to Cairns and a mysterious place called 'ZES' or the 'house on the hill'.

As Carse was winging his way north to Cairns and his new home at the 'Z' Experimental Station, the *Krait*, with her highly trained but somewhat motley eight-man crew, was steaming northwards in between breakdowns. The crew was eventually transferred to the secret ZES training camp where Carse was by then well established as part of the training team. He had been waiting patiently on news about a 'show' that was being planned when he was summoned by Captain Lyon and told that they would like him to navigate the *Krait*. Its destination was still a closely guarded secret but he was ordered to go over the vessel with a fine-tooth comb and to ensure that she was not only seaworthy, but that she could carry enough fuel to travel 13,000 nautical miles (just over 24,000 kilometres). Such a figure hardly narrowed down the possibilities, because that was enough juice to power the boat all the way to Great Britain.

Finally, Lyon revealed the true nature of the operation to the officers Ted Carse and Bob Page.

'We propose to attack Japanese shipping in Singapore harbour and to get there and back in the *Krait*,' Lyon explained. 'If we can't return to Australia we may have to head for Africa or even Pearl Harbor and that's why we must have long range.'

Lyon would be in command. Lieutenant Davidson would be both his 2IC and the commander of the attack party that would paddle into Singapore harbour and set magnetic limpet mines on the hulls of as many ships as possible. Lyon also told them that the name of the operation had been changed from 'Jock Force' to 'Jaywick'.

A stunned Carse went to the slipway at Stratford Bridge on the Barron River north of Cairns to conduct his survey of the *Krait* and was scared stiff by what he found. The plan to take her to Singapore appeared to be totally insane.

He had first laid eyes on the old fishing boat soon after she arrived in Cairns under tow with Paddy McDowell in command. When Carse had asked McDowell what he called his strange-looking craft he replied, 'A real bastard.'

McDowell had explained that her engine had already stopped about 10 times on the journey north from Sydney and that she was named *Krait* after a venomous Indian snake, but 'if you asked me, I'd spell the bastard C-R-A-T-E'.

The two men who would work closely to keep the old girl operating during the mission hit it off just fine. Like Ted Carse, the 56-year-old McDowell had done a stint in the navy, rising to the rank of petty officer. He had settled in Sydney from his native Belfast and was in the Royal Navy Reserve when World War II broke out. He had joined the RAN as a leading stoker and, as Carse told McKie, he had never met anyone more imperturbable than Paddy McDowell.

Carse was also deeply impressed by the gentle and sensitive Lieutenant Bob Page who was a graduate of Sydney High School and a second-year medical student when war broke out. His father, Harold Page, had been awarded the Distinguished Service Order (DSO) and Military Cross (MC), as well as three Mentioned in Dispatches (MIDs) in World War I, and his uncle was the politician Sir Earle Page.

Lieutenant Page knew that his father had been taken prisoner by the Japanese at Rabaul, but he did not know that he had perished, along with 1000 other souls, when the Japanese prison ship *Montevideo Maru* was sunk by the American submarine USS *Sturgeon* off the Philippines on 1 July 1942.

'A man must be ready not only to fight,' Page told Carse, 'but to give his life and to give it gladly.'

This was an admirable sentiment, but for Carse the reality of preparing a small Japanese fishing boat for an arduous journey deep behind enemy lines and then home again was almost fanciful.

The more he thought about Singapore, the more convinced he became that no member of the raiding party would even see Singapore let alone survive the mission. And yet as a volunteer he had accepted the risk, so on he pushed.

Ted Carse has since been criticised in some quarters not only for his 'heavy' drinking but also for his alleged harsh approach to his crew. However, Horrie Young also rejected this view of Carse, the man to whom he was closest throughout the mission.

'I don't believe I can ever recall Carse wasting a word. His knowledge of the sea was most extensive,' Young said. 'He could "read" the weather signs with uncanny accuracy and if he said there was bad weather afoot you could bet your life that he was correct. His seamanship was beyond reproach. I never ever heard him admonish anybody. He was seen to be so understanding, you know, and he had so many things that were pluses in my view.

'His eyes were like red meat sort of thing, and he suffered also from … huge lumps of fluid on his elbows, which were extremely painful, but never once did I ever hear him complain. He never whinged about this, although it was quite apparent that he was in considerable pain. I think I can confidently say that he was an inspiration to all of us.'

In January 2018 Moss Berryman described Carse, who was christened the 'Admiral' by his shipmates, as a quiet bloke who occasionally fired up when he was arguing with his fellow officers.

'He was relied upon heavily while we were away because it is pretty treacherous country there above Indonesia,' Berryman said.

Ted Carse was awarded an MID in April 1944 'For gallantry, skill and devotion to duty in a hazardous enterprise.'

Once they had unloaded the raiding team of the six canoeists and their supplies, it was Carse's responsibility to take the *Krait* back to sea while they cruised around the islands of the archipelago for 14 tense days.

'We just went around and around in circles and we all got on well including him,' Berryman said. 'There were no arguments at all. It is tricky around those islands at times, and you are doing a few left and right turns.'

'Tricky' is an understatement for the skilful way Carse skippered the *Krait* in and out of the inlets and islands. The remaining crew on board had no idea whether they would ever see their shipmates again or whether at any time they would be intercepted by a Japanese patrol, which would have led to their capture, torture and almost certain execution.

'I consider it to be to his great credit that he was able to navigate *Krait* from Australia to the islands nominated by the canoeists,' said Young. 'Take the vessel across busy sea-lanes, undetected, to the coast of Borneo and skilfully conceal her from harm and then return her by the same course to the pick-up point. Truly a remarkable feat when one considers that he was the only officer on board with a reduced crew and minimal firepower and at the same time suffering severely from the effects of eyestrain along with other painful disabilities.'

Young, who had built his first radio set aged 11 years and had enlisted in the navy at 16, joined the *Krait* in Cairns and was immediately impressed by the camaraderie of the Jaywick team. As he installed and fine-tuned his radio equipment he observed his shipmates running barefoot along the beach, wrestling and paddling the folboats in the open sea.

'Davidson and Lyon had certainly chosen the team most carefully and the results were obvious,' Young wrote in his diary. 'They were indeed a grand team, fun to be with and totally compatible with each other.'

He also described Berryman as a willing and reliable operative. 'He was well liked and always ready to help out with any task.'

Poppa Falls, he said, was a large, tough lad of Scottish ancestry whose years on the family dairy farm had hardened him up and made him a natural for the raid. Falls would share a canoe with Lieutenant Davidson.

'Joe' Jones had served in the armed merchant cruiser HMAS *Manoora* prior to volunteering for special duty. Young described him as an experienced able seaman who knew his way around ships and was a very reliable helmsman. Jones would share a canoe with Lieutenant Page.

At 18, 'Happy' Huston was the baby of the team. His nickname derived from the fact that he seldom smiled. Horrie Young described him as a 'diligent' and 'hardworking' member of the crew. He was Lyon's canoe partner for the attack.

The second reserve canoeist was 'Boof' Marsh. According to Young, Marsh was the light-hearted member of the party and was never happier than when he was playing practical jokes on his shipmates.

The powerfully built Cobber Cain was a professional navy man and had served at sea for most of the war before joining Jaywick. Cain was considerably older than the others (except McDowell) and was appointed coxswain for the mission.

Then there was Taffy Morris, Ivan Lyon's Welsh batman and the ship's medic. His sonorous voice, straight out of the Welsh valleys, and his bubbly personality were a source of joy for his shipmates throughout the long journey.

4

Getting to know her

Another vital piece of the puzzle was also waiting in Cairns – a near-new engine.

The British-built Gardner 6L3 103 horsepower diesel engine was purchased from Tasmanian timber company AG Webster and Sons for £2250 and flown north to replace the unreliable German-made Deutz motor that had failed them numerous times during the long journey from Singapore to India and on the passage north from Broken Bay. The Gardner diesel is regarded as one of the world's greatest boat motors and many are still powering vessels around the world.

As well as the Gardner diesel, the boat was equipped with a single-cylinder British-made Ruston-Hornsby petrol motor to power the air compressor that was used to start the main engine. The compressed air is pumped into the Gardner to push the cylinders down and get her kicking over. Once the engine fires it's decompressed with a distinctive 'choo choo' sound.

In addition to the engine, the consignment included a package of 41 spare parts such as fuel pumps, piston guides, water connecting tubes and starting handles. More spares that would be required for the engine included cylinder liners, bearings, couplings, injectors, gaskets, rings and valves. All of this would need to be acquired and sent to Cairns or Exmouth before the operation commenced.

As an army engineer, Andy Crilly took more than a passing interest in the engine. He was also in awe of the ability of Paddy McDowell to maintain machinery.

'We must mention the engine room which housed the greatest motor ever made and we are proud to say that it was British,' Crilly's account says.

One piece of equipment that was fitted on top of the *Krait*'s radio console would be a constant reminder of the gravity of the mission – a large carton containing about 70 kilograms of plastic 808 explosive that was located about 30 centimetres from Horrie Young's face as he sat at his radio set.

The cortex (high speed fuse) that would be used to detonate the device in the event that the *Krait* was intercepted by a Japanese warship, was draped across his operating table and ran to a point under Lyon's bunk where an instantaneous detonator was fitted. In the event of imminent capture, the plan was that Lyon would blow the *Krait*, her complement and, he hoped, the enemy vessel to kingdom come.

When Young first set eyes on the *Krait* in Cairns he, like others in the team, was shocked that such a tiny vessel would be home to himself and his 13 shipmates for the foreseeable future.

'I had spent virtually all of my previous sea time on small ships, minesweepers, etc., which are often lacking in typical navy spit and polish, and with all the usual discomforts, cramped accommodation, bad food and frequent bouts of sea sickness, I had never before seen anything quite as bad as the *Krait*,' he wrote later.

Nor had he ever met anyone quite like leading stoker Paddy McDowell, who emerged from the bowels of the vessel rolling a customary cigarette and introducing himself as the ship's engineer. He guided Horrie on a tour of the boat and introduced him to his 3 by 2.5-metre radio shack that would double as the operations centre and living quarters for three officers.

'Also in attendance were hordes of some of the largest cockroaches the like of which I had never seen before,' Young wrote. 'These creatures remained on board for the entire voyage, notwithstanding that the vessel was allegedly fumigated prior to our departure. It seems as though they must have taken shore leave during the fumigation process and returned prior to sailing.'

Young also recalled that Lieutenant Davidson's courage was constantly on display as he honed his hand-to-hand combat skills and came up with various new and bizarre methods of dealing with the enemy. One of his most imaginative ideas was for a miniature attack or 'stealth' dinghy to be deployed should an enemy vessel intercept the *Krait*.

Young described the contraption as a 'Heath Robinson' idea, after the British illustrator whose drawings of complicated and implausible machines became popular during World War I.

Davidson wanted to equip the ship's dinghy with air pipes that were fitted through the seats and the hull and attached to a gas mask underneath the boat. According to Davidson's scenario, Arthur 'Joe' Jones, who was the darkest-skinned of the Jaywick team, would don a large hat and then paddle towards the enemy vessel with empty water containers pleading for 'water! water!'. Meanwhile, Davidson would be fastened to the underside of the dinghy by leather straps and breathing through the gas mask. He would carry two powerful magnetic limpet mines on very short fuses that he would attach to the hull of the enemy vessel. The idea was that once the mines were attached and Davidson was back underneath, Jones would then paddle like hell away from the point of detonation.

'Fortunately, we didn't have to test it or put the thing into practice but that gives you some idea of what Davidson was like. He was always thinking up new ideas,' Young wrote.

Horrie Young's son Brian, who was born just as the Jaywick team left Australia, said his father regarded the *Krait* as the happiest vessel he ever served in. 'And he was on an awful lot of warships. He was on minesweepers and destroyers, cruisers, all sorts of things. So he certainly had an attachment to the *Krait*.'

As departure day approached, Carse noticed that the normally intense Ivan Lyon (by then promoted to major) had become even more focused, more distant and more impersonal. This anxiety is perfectly understandable given the gravity of the mission he was about to lead and the fact that his wife and infant son were in enemy hands, and might even be imprisoned in the very city that he was planning to attack.

Ted Carse and the others believed that Ivan Lyon was not a man whom anyone would ever know well.

'Lyon was always a little apart and others were conscious of his aloofness and of the barrier he erected and stayed behind,' Carse told Ronald McKie. 'He could be friendly, charming and yet he lacked warmth, lacked those touches of personality which make others feel that here is a man who recognises and understands them as feeling, suffering human beings.'

As June gave way to July, Carse became immersed in the logistics of the upcoming voyage. But he noticed that Lyon was seldom still, ate little and slept even less, and the only time he appeared to relax was over a beer or two with dinner.

Krait would carry four months worth of supplies and the skipper had to know what and where every single item was, from the Bren machine guns to the 'L' cyanide suicide pills that would be kept by Lyon and issued if capture was imminent.

Operational supplies for the six-man raiding party were stored in sealed tins, which each contained enough food and canned heat to supply four men for four days. The essential items included tinned meat, condensed milk tablets, chocolate, biscuits, peanuts, sweets, cigarettes, matches and a paperback novel. Distilled water was carried in one- and two-gallon tins. Medical stores included medicinal rum, gin and whisky as well as lime juice, vitamins, Atabrine, an anti-malarial drug, quinine and a first-aid kit complete with morphine and syringes.

The *Krait* also carried 50,000 cigarettes (mainly for trading), £200 in Dutch guilders, two Lewis guns, two Bren guns, eight Sten guns, eight Owen submachine guns, 14 Smith & Wesson revolvers, 200 hand grenades, stabbing knives, throwing knives, jungle parangs, 45 limpet mines and 150 pounds (70 kilograms) of plastic explosive – enough to sink about 15 ships.

Many Japanese-made items were also carried including sunglasses, toothbrushes and pots and pans, to avoid suspicion in case anything went overboard.

While the new Gardner engine was being fitted, Carse was ordered to fly to Melbourne for a final briefing from Cocky Long and to collect the latest navigation charts from the Dutch commander of Allied naval forces in the Pacific, Admiral Conrad Helfrich. The admiral, who had been in command of Dutch forces in the Netherlands East Indies since 1939, advised Carse that the best hiding place for the *Krait* would be up one of the rivers along the coast of Sumatra where overhanging palm trees would conceal her from view. In the event, this proved to be a suggestion that, although well intentioned, could have led to disaster for the boat and her crew as enemy vessels conducted regular patrols of the inlets. Remaining on the move would be the safer option.

Late July was frantic at the 'house on the hill' as Lyon and Davidson finalised the operational details of the mission and Carse, McDowell and Cain scoured the *Krait* to ensure that she was in tip-top condition for the arduous voyage ahead. Horrie Young was kept busy setting up and tuning the barely adequate communications equipment provided to the vessel.

The new Gardner engine now installed, the team set off for Townsville on 4 August on a shakedown cruise to collect vital stores and navigation equipment.

Lieutenant Davidson's log, held by the National Archives of Australia, records that the weather on 5 August was fine and calm. 'Owing to not having yet picked up our navigational instruments, navigation was a series of point-to-point coasting. Speed seven knots.'

Early next morning they arrived at the entrance to Townsville Roads. (A 'road' is a sheltered anchorage or roadstead at the entrance to a harbour). 'Speed was reduced to slow, and we zig-zagged until dawn when we proceeded to Townsville.'

By 7.30 am they were berthed at Harbour Board wharf and they spent the day loading up stores. 'Navigational instruments arrived, except the azimuth mirror.' This is a navigational mirror that allows the observer to see both a compass and an object such as a star at the same time and in the same direction.

On 8 August they set off back to Cairns at seven knots in fine and calm conditions with a light southeasterly blowing.

Arriving in Cairns early on Monday, 9 August, they spent the day undertaking minor repairs, taking on a spare propeller and a new dinghy and 'tarring' the sail and all hemp ropes – applying tar to prevent rotting.

'Ship was filthy on completion, but there was no time to clean her before sailing,' Davidson noted. At 10.30 pm the *Krait* set off, bound for Thursday Island.

It was exactly 18 months to the day since Ivan Lyon and Taffy Morris had sailed from Padang in Sumatra for Ceylon (Sri Lanka) and Donald Davidson had departed Sandakan in Borneo in a small boat to sail to Australia.

Lieutenant Ted Carse took the MV *Krait* and his 13 shipmates quietly out of Cairns harbour and around Ellie Point. They were heading for Exmouth at the top of Western Australia, more than 2000 nautical miles (3800 kilometres) to the north and west on the first leg of their incredible adventure. For Carse, the eight months since his 'interview' with the strange Colonel Mott in Melbourne had passed in the blink of an eye.

Twenty-year-old Berryman regarded the 12 months since he had blindly volunteered for 'special service', and had been put through his paces by the tough men in the sandhills at the commando training school in Frankston, as a huge adventure. Never in his wildest dreams could he have imagined when he signed on for navy duty back in Adelaide that he would be sailing from Cairns in a wooden fishing boat on a top-secret mission and bound for an unknown destination.

During his time at the 'house on the hill' Berryman had met young men from Timor and the Philippines who were also being trained, before being dropped back into their own countries to take the fight to the Japanese. He had also learned the dark arts of commando operations and the importance of stealth and surprise.

During one training operation at the Cairns aerodrome Berryman and two others had marched in right behind the guards and 'tagged' several aircraft.

'We went up into the tower and the chap up there was sound asleep,' he recalled. 'So we jammed a few things against the door so he couldn't get out, just for the fun of it, and nobody was caught, so we got in a truck and went back to our house on the hill.'

The next day an air force officer arrived at the camp. 'We took a look at him and thought, "We're going to cop it now", but he was so friendly. He said, "This is what I've been trying to tell the authorities – it's going to happen sooner or later, and you boys have done it. I'm pleased".'

As the *Krait* set a course for Cooktown, Cape Melville and Thursday Island, Moss Berryman must have wondered what surprises the next phase of the great adventure would hold.

5

The Douglas effect

As the youngest son of a World War I veteran from a modest family in Alstonville in northern New South Wales, Douglas Herps well understood the meaning and cost of war, and the value of a penny. So when an offer came his way to earn an extra four shillings a day once he was parachute-qualified, and 12 shillings a day if and when he was deployed, he jumped at the chance to join a top-secret 'special' unit. At the time, the entirety of his army wage of six shillings a day was being paid directly to his mother so the opportunity to double it was too good to refuse and he joined 'Z' Special Unit.

At a secret camp on Fraser Island in Queensland, Herps was trained in a variety of commando skills, ranging from paddling canvas-covered folboats to packing and handling a packhorse, speaking the Malay language, handling explosives and lethal unarmed combat.

The folboats were used for numerous operations – not just Jaywick – and later in the war they were deployed from both submarines and snake boats. The snake boats were armed, 80-tonne vessels specially designed for 'Z' Special Unit to resemble a Malay fishing boat and were used to secretly deliver and retrieve operatives. But despite all the training, Douglas Herps never deployed in a folboat in anger. Instead, he was parachuted behind enemy lines into Borneo for one of the missions codenamed 'Agas' in 1945.

However, during one training mission he and several of his mates paddled 20 kilometres up the Mary River to conduct a simulated attack against a shipyard near Maryborough. They managed to lay their dummy charges and escape before the shipbuilders turned up for work, discovered the 'charges' and fled the scene in terror. In typical 'Z' fashion even the local police weren't informed until after the event.

Douglas Herps's crusade to honour his dead mates and other unknown former colleagues began at the Commonwealth War Cemetery in Labuan, Borneo, when he and his wife, Patricia, were on a cruising holiday. He took a photo of the headstone of a 'Z' Special operative and sent it to the man's family who'd had no idea where he was buried or how he had died.

That simple act triggered a 15-year odyssey to track down and photograph the graves of as many operatives as he could.

'That was purely to honour his mates so they would be remembered, and to remind governments so that they might avoid conflicts in the future,' his elder son, Jonathan, said during a 2017 interview.

The headstone mission morphed into a quest to preserve the MV *Krait* as a sacred memorial to members of 'Z' Special Unit and the other secret warriors of World War II.

'Dad thought it was important to make *Krait* a memorial to all special forces and to create a museum because the public can't get into Holsworthy (Commando) or Swanbourne (SAS) barracks to see the major museums. He was seeing *Krait* decaying and he wasn't going to allow her to sink out of sight. It became his passion and he spent many years pursuing anybody. Thank goodness for the ANMM, because it saved the boat and a lot of time and money has been spent by the museum,' Jonathan added.

When Douglas Herps put his mind to the permanent preservation of the *Krait*, during the 1990s he was initially in favour of transporting it to a purpose-built facility at the AWM in Canberra and he drafted some heavy hitters in support of his position. The AWM has owned the *Krait* since the mid-1980s.

He even wrote to British royals Prince William and Prince Harry, inviting them to inspect the *Krait* during their Australian tours. Prince William and the Duchess of Cambridge had made a special pilgrimage to the graves of 'Z' Special Unit operatives buried at Kranji War Cemetery in Singapore, where 4461 Allied personnel are interred. The two princes, both of whom have served in the British armed forces, are said to be very familiar with the stories of Operations Jaywick and Rimau.

Herps, who was promoted to sergeant in 'Z' Special Unit at the tender age of 21 and was wounded in action during a clandestine mission in Borneo, commissioned numerous studies into the vessel and sought opinions from everyone from paint-makers to curators and academics to shipwrights regarding options for her preservation. The overwhelming view was that logistically, moving the boat to Canberra was feasible.

In November 2010, the late naval architect and boatbuilder Warwick Hood told him that the vessel was suitable for transportation and display at the AWM under certain conditions.

Hood outlined those conditions in a brief report to Herps. They included protecting the boat from the elements, making her rodent-proof and displaying her in a substantial cradle based on a steel beam running the full length of the vessel's keel.

'It is expected that a member of the memorial's curatorial staff having experience with the preservation of large wooden artefacts, e.g. a Mosquito aircraft, be appointed to be responsible for the MV *Krait*,' the report noted.

In a letter to Douglas Herps dated 13 April 2011, the manager of the Newcastle Maritime Centre and Museum, Richard Howard, agreed that it was possible to successfully transfer the craft to Canberra from a wet to a dry environment: 'We believe that it would be advisable that you dry the craft slowly, damping down as it dries to avoid cracking and that at all times your craft is cradled in such a way as to avoid breaking its back.'

Herps even had a trucking company lined up to transport the vessel down the Hume Highway. Yet despite his hard work and lobbying, the push to display *Krait* in Canberra ran out of steam.

There were two principal reasons. For decades, feelings had run high against the idea that *Krait*'s final resting place should be in the national capital, hundreds of kilometres away from the coast and her natural maritime environment. Then there were practical reasons, not least being the fact that the AWM had nowhere to house such a large exhibit.

'Our problem here with the Australian War Memorial, as I say to the navy, is that their stuff is so big,' the director Brendan Nelson said in his large office inside the AWM's fortress-like administrative building. 'Once *Krait* comes out of the water it's out – and we have no space for it here. We do have well-developed plans for expansion of the Australian War Memorial but ... I could not justify the amount of space that the *Krait* itself would take.

'We have a model of it and a display of Z Special and so on here, but you couldn't justify the opportunity costs of the exhibition space involved in the *Krait* here, where we are a war memorial which covers all of our conflicts, our three services and so on. Whereas the maritime museum is specifically a maritime museum.'

Once it became apparent that exhibiting *Krait* in the AWM was out of the question, Herps shifted gear and moved his focus to first having the vessel restored to her 1943 configuration and then to achieving a permanent out-of-water display at the ANMM. He also convinced Dr Nelson of the need for a stakeholder survey to gauge the views of everyone with an interest in the vessel, such as veterans' groups, former users, historians, naval architects, the museums and modern-day special forces as well as the wider Australian Defence Force (ADF).

Most agreed that the *Krait* should be preserved either in the water or in a purpose-built facility on land, but opinions were strongly divided about which was the better option.

The assistant director, national collection, at the AWM, Major General (retired) Brian 'Smokey' Dawson, said he was amazed to discover that 60 per cent of the teak planks in the *Krait* were original.

'Up until then I had kind of had the view that in one sense it was like Grandpa's axe, with two new handles and three new heads, but it was actually quite a long way from that. The engine that was put in, I think, in 1943 is still the engine that's in there,' he said. 'It's a very understated boat, and … I'm sure there are thousands of people who walk past it without giving it a second thought. But if you know the story and you know where it's been and what it's done, [you realise that] it's just a remarkable piece of Australian military history and … where it sits in Darling Harbour exposed to lots of the public, I can't think of a better place for it.'

ANMM director Kevin Sumption was another who came under the Herps spell and he praises the 'Z' Special Unit veteran's commitment to the campaign to have the *Krait* ultimately preserved on dry land and in a special facility at the museum.

'My hope is that in the next five to ten years we can make the transition out of the water into a purpose-built facility that will also allow it to continue to operate as a memorial to commemorate service ... the drive for that is very much due to Douglas Herps,' he said during an interview in his office overlooking Darling Harbour. 'You run a big museum like this; there are 140,000 objects, there are many things going on and Douglas's very strong case that, "Yes, there are 139,999 other objects but this one needs special attention" – I have to pay him the ultimate compliment and say that the work that is happening here now is very much his legacy, is very much what he pushed for and is quite rightfully going forward.'

Sumption is also mindful of the fact that the *Krait* is used as the focal point for solemn Remembrance Day services by elements of the special forces community.

'It's an important function, but it also has an impact upon the authenticity and the originality of the vessel. The longer it stays in the water the less of the original fabric – not only of the 1934 fishing vessel but the 1943 vessel – is there because the mere fact it is sitting in the water means eventually timbers get saturated, [become] affected by the environment and they ultimately will need to be replaced. In the short term, being in the water doesn't present too many difficulties that we're not able to handle but the museum's business is in perpetuity,' he said.

'I am trusted for a very brief time as a custodian of an object that ultimately, in 200, 300, 400 years, we want to know that's still with us, that the story is still able to be told. So, that's a very long timeframe but it's the timeframe that museums do work in. When you look through that timeframe, there's no doubt the vessel needs to be out of the water – because in that timeframe there will be nothing left of the original vessel.'

Like many children of war veterans, Jonathan and Nicholas Herps knew little of their father's wartime activities as they were growing up. The subject was quickly changed whenever the Herps brothers posed the classic question, 'What did you do in the war, Dad?'

They didn't even know that he had been wounded in action until a grown-up Nicholas noticed a fairly large scar on his father's leg.

'What happened there, Dad?' he asked.

'Oh, that's just where a Jap stuck me with a dagger,' was the only response the gobsmacked son received.

Douglas later explained that the enemy soldier was the biggest 'Jap' he had ever seen during his time behind enemy lines in Borneo. He also made it clear to his sons that direct contact with the enemy was not the main objective for him and his fellow operatives working alongside native forces.

Both Herps's sons have played an active role in the *Krait* project and they understand the profound importance that their father attached to the old Japanese fishing boat. The family trust also donated $50,000 to the preservation fund.

'It was his deathbed wish that we save the *Krait*,' Jonathan said. 'I don't think Dad wanted to share the journey. It was something he wanted to do for his mates. He didn't want my help at the time and that was frustrating. He wanted to do it himself. Eventually he said to us that he wanted us to carry on.'

Jonathan, who served in the Army Reserves and was an aide-de-camp to the late New South Wales governor, Air Marshal Sir

James Rowland, believes that his father suffered from undiagnosed post-traumatic stress (PTS) for many years.

'Dad never spoke about the war, his involvement or what he did. He never marched on Anzac Day and never went to reunions because he thought the cooks and bottle washers were running the show. I think he had PTSD or PTS all his postwar life.'

'He didn't speak about operations in any detail,' said Nicholas. 'The attrition rate was so high that talking about it brought back bad memories.'

He said his father would be very proud of the way the shipwrights and their apprentices had refurbished the vessel and very proud of the dedicated team who have carried on the tradition of the *Krait*.

Herps would also be proud of the work done by his sons and by others in keeping the flame burning. For example, Jonathan lobbied the then Chief of the Defence Force Air Chief Marshal Mark Binskin in 2016 and his efforts, supported by Brendan Nelson, resulted in a $500,000 contribution by the then Chief of Army and former Special Air Service Regiment (SAS) officer Lieutenant General Angus Campbell to the *Krait* restoration fund.

Nicholas said his father told him that although the *Krait* was just an old fishing boat with no value to anyone, to him and his mates it was a memorial. 'As he got older that feeling became more pronounced.'

Douglas Herps had limited formal schooling but his intelligence shone through in many ways, from learning the complete works of William Shakespeare off by heart to becoming a very successful postwar property developer.

'He had tunnel vision with everything that he did and the *Krait* was the thing that he devoted his life towards in the later stages of his life. His tunnel vision just focused on that,' Nicholas said. 'If he was still alive, he would be happy with the progress, but he would be saying, "That's great, but it's only a start, so get on with it!" He saw going to war as a public service and he thought the same about the *Krait*.'

The ANMM 2016 vessel management plan states that the *Krait* and her Japanese-built sister ships illustrated the strong influence of British boatbuilding techniques on Far-Eastern fleets:

> *Krait* is the last remaining example of Japanese adaptation of the English drift netter [seine boat] for their use. While 21st century society is persuaded to the concept of planned obsolescence, *Krait* represents the opposite – it was designed and built in a manner that allowed it to serve effectively in a range of roles beyond its original use for fishing. It may have been used for Japanese military surveillance while it was fishing, however it did operate subsequently as a wartime rescue boat, transport for sabotage operations, a timber carrier and tugboat, then finally a coast guard vessel before becoming a museum vessel.
>
> The boat is very relevant to the history of Singapore, having operated from there for seven years prior to the war, and then having had its major operational success in the raid on Singapore's port. This raid however resulted in the internment, torture and death of some of the local citizens, and it is a powerful reminder of the consequences of war.

Douglas Herps was deeply moved by the fate of the innocents in Singapore and his intense lobbying began to pay off as he approached the end of his life. Not only had he convinced both the *Krait*'s owner, the AWM, and her custodian, the ANMM, of the urgency and importance of ensuring the boat's long-term preservation, but he had developed a network of people to carry on his work after he was gone.

The traditions of Operation Jaywick and the MV *Krait* run deep in the modern-day special forces community. As the vessel management plan states, 'Vessels with the provenance of *Krait* are rare with no known examples in collections. Very little remains to reflect the sabotage operations of Special Services during the Second World War; as a means of insertion of operatives for a classic canoe raid *Krait* is unique.'

Ninety-one-year-old Douglas Herps died peacefully in Sydney on 23 April 2015 but not before the Governor General Sir Peter Cosgrove attended his bedside to bestow the Order of Australia Medal on him. His legacy lives on and his dream to have the *Krait* displayed out of the water for once and for all remains squarely in the sights of both the AWM and the ANMM.

THE
SINGAPORE
TERROR

6

To Lombok Strait

With her new Gardner diesel engine purring sweetly, the *Krait* chugged slowly northwards towards the tip of Cape York Peninsula.

As the four soldiers and 10 sailors settled into their routines, no one aboard any vessel that passed the foreign-looking fishing boat could, in their wildest dreams, have imagined where she was heading or what her mission was.

Of the 10 navy men in the *Krait* only four – Carse, McDowell, Cain and Jones – had any seagoing or watch-keeping experience at all. There is a world of difference between sailing small boats around the islands of the South China Sea or canoeing through the jungle or across Broken Bay and navigating a vessel on the high seas.

Ted Carse was the one man formally qualified to skipper the vessel to Singapore and back and only stoker Paddy McDowell could keep her engines running and the boat seaworthy, with army motor mechanic Andy 'Pancake' Crilly as backup.

The first two days of the voyage, 10 and 11 August, were uneventful as they motored north through the hazardous but calm waters of the Great Barrier Reef at just above six knots. Then, at 2.30 am on 12 August, the boat shuddered and scraped as she ran aground at about three knots close to Chapman Island between Cape Melville and Cape York.

'02.30: Ran onto coral shelf in the vicinity of Chapman Is.,' Davidson wrote in the official log of the first stage of the voyage. 'Without an Azimuth Mirror navigation is difficult in these waters. Speed three knots at the time.'

Carse backed her off the reef in about 30 minutes and anchored in deeper water nearby to assess the damage. Fortunately, none was done. The *Krait*'s teak hull remained watertight and her four holds secure.

The boat was heavily laden. Number 4 hold, just below the wheelhouse, contained her main diesel fuel supply, while number 3 hold, which housed Horrie Young's radio shack, was also the officers' quarters as well as holding enough explosive 'to blow up half of Sydney', as Young put it. Number 2 hold contained the food supplies and number 1, at the bow, the limpet mines and hand grenades. She also carried fishing nets.

Weapons and ammunition were stored in an easily accessible waterproof box stowed on top of the engine room hatch just aft of the wheelhouse. An extra eight 44-gallon (166-litre) drums of diesel were lashed to the deck along with eight 4-gallon (15-litre) drums of petrol to power the auxiliary motor, known as 'Mickey Mouse', that provided light and compressed air for starting for the main engine.

Indeed, the *Krait* was so weighed down, Horrie Young commented in his diary that the vessel sat so low in the water you could 'sit on the gunwale and dip your dinner plate in the sea'.

Three officers – Lyon, Davidson and Page – slept in number 3 hold, Carse slept in the wheelhouse and McDowell bunked next to his beloved engine. The nine other ranks slept where they could find a space and ate under the canvas-covered aft section between the wheelhouse and the galley, which consisted of a small primus stove and some shelves.

Such close quarters meant that the men had to get on with each other so that aspect of their characters had been studied closely during Lyon and Davidson's gruelling selection process.

Both Horrie Young and Moss Berryman agreed that all 14 men did indeed get along very well and there was barely a cross word spoken during the entire journey, despite the fact that they were living in a space not much bigger than a modern-day suburban lounge room. When they were not on watch the men spent their time sleeping, maintaining equipment, reading or playing cribbage.

The vessel operated under four-hour watches with an officer at the helm at all times and one lookout amidships, another at the stern and a third aloft on the mast around the clock. The masthead watch was relieved every hour and was vital in extending the low-riding boat's outlook by several kilometres.

The *Krait* docked at Thursday Island off the northern tip of Australia on Friday, 13 August 1943.

'Arrived Thursday Is.,' Davidson recorded. 'Berthed inside eastern arm of jetty. Received onward route from N.C.S.O. [national chief signal officer] and later intelligence summary. Air cover was arranged with RAAF Horn Is. Postponed sailing, today being Black Friday, until morning.'

While Carse wanted to depart the same day, the deeply superstitious Lyon insisted that they wait until the next day. Carse would later tell Ronald McKie his concerns about Lyon's superstitious nature. Back at the 'house on the hill' Carse and Davidson had casually mentioned that they were going to win a fortune in the lottery and Lyon had exploded.

'If you win anything in that lottery I am not going on the raid,' he snapped. 'If you are lucky with money you can't be lucky in war. It just isn't possible.'

Lyon had also become irritable and jumpy when, off Cooktown, the crew witnessed a pod of killer whales attacking a larger whale. The *Krait* had motored through a cauldron of bloody froth as the huge, wounded mammal attempted in vain to evade its attackers.

As the boat motored west towards Exmouth Gulf at a steady six knots and in a rising swell, the crew settled in to their watch-keeping routine. Approaching the Wessel Islands off the northeastern tip of Arnhem Land the crew went to action stations when a bright light flash was spotted high in the sky.

It turned out to be an astronomical false alarm – a very bright Venus – but it was a reminder that they were traversing an area where Japanese bombers operated regularly and where enemy aircraft had sunk a freighter just a month earlier.

They were called to 'action stations' several more times when aircraft were spotted, but the planes proved to be Beaufort light bombers providing friendly cover, according to Davidson's log.

With a blocked filter fixed and Cape Wessel abeam, Davidson noted on 16 August that their route took them to within 20 miles (32 kilometres) of the coast for air protection from the Royal Australian Air Force's (RAAF's) Spitfire Squadron based on Milingimbi Island. An unidentified aircraft, thought to be friendly, was also spotted some 10 kilometres away.

On 17 August, Lyon's twenty-eighth birthday, Davidson noted. 'Passed a seagull riding on a turtle's back. Saw quite a number of turtles that day.'

On the same day, Lyon's superstitious side was tested once more when Cobber Cain was cleaning a Lewis gun and a round discharged, smashing a tomato sauce bottle on its way out of the deck space. Fortunately, no one was too seriously hurt but Taffy Morris copped a piece of glass in his ankle that cut the artery – so a flow of blood replaced the tomato sauce that had sprayed everywhere.

The former medical student, Bob Page, staunched the wound but for the rest of the mission Morris had a pronounced limp. The incident evoked a deeper level of melancholy in Lyon who told Carse that luck appeared to be 'dead against us'.

The cynical old sea dog said nothing but had a laugh later that day when at, 4.45 pm, with Lyon at the helm, the boat scraped a sandbar at the northern extremity of Mermaid Shoal. Fortunately, there was no damage. Carse also had a quiet chuckle two days later when the sea around the *Krait* came alive with swarms of crabs mixed with dozens of evil-looking, mustard-coloured sea snakes.

But Lyon's mood brightened soon afterwards when some sixth sense told Carse to alter course due to danger ahead. As daylight broke it was evident that the vessel had been on a direct collision course with a reef. Had the skipper not turned during the night she would almost certainly have foundered. According to Lyon at least, the mission's luck had turned and would now be on their side.

However, luck had nothing to do with a decision he soon had to make when the boat approached the Montebello Islands to the north of Exmouth in heavy seas.

On 23 August, Davidson recorded: 'An unpleasant sea is running from the [south], on our beam. Ran into a bad rip on the 100-fathom line, with heavy confused seas dominated by a heavy swell. It was out of the question to hold our course … *Krait* rolling her lee scuppers under and finding it hard to shake herself free again.'

In Cairns, Lyon had ordered a protective coating of a tar-like bulletproof material to be laid across the deck, but on top of her huge load of supplies it had made the vessel top heavy and she was burying her head in the rising sea. With the rough seas continuing, Carse told Lyon that the 2.5 tons of bitumen would have to go. Somewhat to Carse's surprise, Lyon agreed immediately and joined the crew in prying it off the deck and throwing it over the side.

The *Krait* reached Exmouth Gulf on 27 August, 18 days after leaving Cairns, and dropped anchor off the United States submarine base known as Potshot.

In his diary, Horrie Young described their stay at Potshot, tied up alongside the American submarine repair ship USS *Chanticleer*, under the command of Captain Hawes, as 'pleasant', but he makes no mention of the excellent American hospitality or of the turkey and cranberry sauce, ice cream or whisky that were supplied by their generous hosts under the command of Rear Admiral Ralph Christie, United States Navy (USN).

Moss Berryman, however, has a clear memory of the Americans' largesse. 'What a glorious life these submarine boys had on this ship,' he said at his home in 2017. 'There was a coffee machine every 20 yards, there was an ice cream machine every 20 yards. They were living on turkey and beef and wonderful food and they said, "Stay on board a few days, enjoy some of our luxury", which we did.'

For the young men who had been living on strictly reduced rations to prepare for the mission, the stay on the American ship was a dream come true.

'When we were back at the Hawkesbury, Captain Lyon said, "Right, we will cut out the midday lunch because where we're going it will be quite a distance and we'd have to be prepared to watch the food very carefully, we don't want to run out",' Berryman recalled. 'So, after spending a week or two at the Hawkesbury without lunch and the same on this long trip from Sydney around to Exmouth with no lunch, you can imagine there was a few grizzles. We're growing boys.'

They were also able to enjoy some leisure time including swimming and walks along the beach, but things suddenly changed when a supply package arrived from Melbourne. It contained numerous items of equipment such as spare parts, compasses, binoculars, a telescope and mail, and the four British-made folboats that were supposed to have been built exactly to Davidson's specifications.

Unfortunately, that was not the case and a furious Davidson and the rest of the raiding party spent the remainder of their downtime at Exmouth modifying the canoes so they would fit together properly. The much-needed azimuth mirror was also missing from the parcel.

Finally the *Krait* was ready to depart from Exmouth, so on the night of 31 August the Americans hosted a farewell party that included some fine Scotch whisky and American bourbon. In return, the Jaywick men presented their hosts with two training canoes, a spare propeller and a compass from the Sultan of Johor's yacht that Captain Bill Reynolds had souvenired back in Singapore.

The next day, as the *Krait* was refuelling from the supply vessel *Ondina Star*, Ivan Lyon received some cables from Melbourne that he had been waiting for. One message announced the safe arrival of Horrie Young's first child, a son called Brian, and that mother and child were doing well. The entire crew gathered around to pat the new dad on the back.

They could now set sail. But as the *Krait* moved away slowly from the *Ondina Star* there was a loud bang from below. A furious Paddy McDowell emerged at the hatch to announce that the coupling key from the intermediate propeller shaft had sheared and the vessel would be unable to move without urgent repairs. Fortunately, the USS *Chanticleer* was still nearby and the *Krait* was towed over to the repair ship, while the crew transferred to the American vessel as the *Krait*'s stern was hoisted clear of the water and the engineers got to work.

They welded the shaft with strict instructions from Captain Hawes that it must be properly repaired when the *Krait* arrived in Fremantle. The Americans believed that was where the vessel was heading.

In his memoir Horrie Young noted many years later, 'It may be of interest to mention that those same repairs remained in place for the next 52 years.'

The propeller shaft, along with its USN weld, was eventually replaced in 1994 by a modern stainless-steel version.

It was 2 pm on 2 September 1943 when Carse announced to Lyon that the shaft had cooled and they were ready to depart.

'Outside the Gulf we ran into a heavy swell and a confused sea from the south, with a fresh south wind,' Davidson recorded in the log. 'We very nearly foundered, but just managed to carry on.'

Carse had ordered that the sail be hoisted but the vessel listed badly to starboard in the heavy seas, with the sail dragging her down. According to Horrie Young's diary she almost capsized before Carse ordered the sail furled and altered course to the north with a following sea.

'It was Ted Carse's skill and seamanship that saved the day on that occasion,' he wrote in his diary.

A 'most secret, to be passed by hand' post-operation Naval Board report on Operation Jaywick held in the National Archives of Australia contains a typescript of Lyon's journal of the voyage from that point.

In it, he noted: 'By nightfall on the 2nd September we were clear of Exmouth Gulf and steering a course to take us about 80 miles west of a direct line between the Gulf and Lombok. A fresh, southerly breeze, which had been blowing for 24 hours, produced an unpleasant sea on our port quarter, giving us our first opportunity to gauge the *Kraits'* qualities as a sea boat in her overloaded state. Despite the removal of the deck armour, she rolled heavily and was distinctly sluggish in her recovery, lying over on one occasion till a man standing beside the wheelhouse found himself waist deep in water.'

He added, 'By morning, conditions had returned to normal and we settled down to the routine of the voyage.'

Towards midday on 3 September, Carse mustered the crew on the forecastle and Lyon stood on the hatch cover below the wheelhouse to announce their destination. Ever since they had been selected for the mission they had been guessing their target and the speculation had ranged from Rabaul to Sumatra and many places in between. One or two, including Joe Jones and Horrie Young, had surmised that Singapore just might be an option.

So by the time Lyon announced that they would be attacking Japanese shipping in Singapore harbour around 25 September nobody was utterly astonished, although the reactions were certainly mixed. Paddy McDowell even claimed to be disappointed, saying that if he had known the target was not Tokyo he would not have volunteered.

Horrie Young, in his diary, simply noted, 'Major Lyon "tells all", not surprised as guessed as much.'

He later expanded on this, saying, 'As I well remember, there was really no reaction to the news that we were bound for Singapore, except perhaps a bit of excitement from the younger members of the crew at the prospect of doing something a bit different from the usual hum-drum shipboard activities.'

He added, 'Taffy Morris, however, later informed me he was somewhat taken aback by the news as he had, not so many months earlier, left Singapore under fairly hazardous circumstances. As for the rest of us, it was "business as usual" as we all went back to our watch-keeping chores.'

Moss Berryman also recalled being a little less than impressed. 'Singapore, in the middle of 1943? We could read a paper and read a map and Singapore at that stage was a long distance, and every part of that world was overrun by Japanese troops. You had the Malay Strait, you had Singapore, Sumatra, Indonesia and Philippines, Timor – and the Japs were sitting up on the top of the Kokoda Trail looking at Australia. Now he tells us we're going to Singapore. "Oh, break it down skipper, that's not a very good idea, is it?" He said, "Yes, it's a good idea, you wait and see". Oh well, too late now to complain, we're miles out to sea and on our way to Singapore.'

Lyon explained that the plan was to attack enemy ships using the canoes and limpet mines and that the raiding party would consist of himself, Davidson, Page, Jones, Falls and Huston. The other two operatives, Boof Marsh and Berryman, protested when they were told they would be held in reserve along with the fourth canoe. They were extremely disappointed to be left behind on the

Krait. Lyon provided few details of the plan in case the mission was compromised before they reached the target.

'We were so trained up we were raring to go even though we were only 18 or 19 in age,' Berryman said.

Lyon also implemented strict security measures that included a ban on smoking and a ban on anything at all going over the side of the boat. That included toilet paper and food scraps or any item at all, no matter how small, that could indicate the presence of Europeans in the area. All rubbish was to be stowed or sunk in perforated metal containers.

Young later wrote, 'The loss of the use of toilet paper was keenly felt by all on board as a bucket of cold sea water is really not a very comfortable or effective substitute – still it was a small sacrifice compared to the risk to our safety and was readily accepted.'

Stringent water restrictions were also imposed for most of the voyage, according to Young. 'Each man was permitted one army canteen bottle of water which had to last three days and was used for all purposes, viz drinking, washing, cleaning teeth, etc. As I recall this was one of our more serious concerns, as all of us seemed to be perpetually thirsty – life in the tropics certainly has that effect. The almost universal use of sea water in preparing our meals tended to compound the problem.'

Fatigue and a lack of concentration were genuine threats to the mission and early the next morning, Paddy McDowell directed Carse's attention to the stern and the pattern of the boat's wake. He had been using the 'head' and had noticed that the wake was bent and the vessel was heading almost due south instead of north. Davidson was at the helm and had lost concentration as he daydreamed about his plan to sink an enemy ship with his newly invented 'attack' dinghy. The *Krait* was actually heading in a slow circle and Carse admonished the mission's 2IC. 'You go and have a good sleep. You'll be better by next watch.'

On 5 September, as they steamed slowly northwards at a steady six knots, the men, for the first time, applied the skin dye that had been provided by the cosmetics firm Helena Rubinstein. It was formulated to make them appear more Asian than European, at least from a distance. It was a disguise that might help to save their lives, and they all understood that – but it didn't stop them grumbling about it.

Davidson wrote, 'Completed painting bodies. The dye is a bad one. Sweat brings it off, any oil does likewise, clothes rub it off. Most unconvincing near to but perhaps effective in general from afar.'

Carse, too, regarded the dye an abject failure, 'The crew now resemble the blackamoors, a more desperate looking crowd I have never seen,' his diary recorded.

On 6 September at 7.30 am Horrie Young ceremoniously replaced the ship's Australian blue ensign with the rising sun ensign of the Empire of Japan. 'But not before we had given it a bath in some of Paddy's diesoline and rubbed it on the deck to give it a well-used appearance.'

Moss Berryman remembered jumping up and down on the flag as well, to make it look more like an authentic, much-used, worn and dirty flag that a fishing boat would fly. From that day onwards sarongs were also the fashion of the day as the men attempted to take on the appearance of local fishermen, at least at a distance. In his diary Young noted that the stained, sarong-wearing men were all 'potential Dorothy Lamours' (an American wartime pin-up girl) and there was much ribald comment. (Later in the voyage, Ted Carse worried that the men would forget themselves when they returned to 'civilisation' and would be arrested for indecent exposure.)

The morning of 8 September dawned with a clear sky and just a few rainy-looking clouds, mostly to eastward. 'These thickened up to 08.30 then cleared to perfection,' Davidson noted. 'Altered course to northward, still at slow speed.'

Lyon wrote, 'The weather during the days of the approach to Lombok was pleasant but we saw nothing of the "very hazy" conditions promised by the Eastern Archipelago pilot. We therefore decided to ignore the threat of air reconnaissance and make a direct approach to the strait entrance.'

They were about to enter one of the most hazardous stretches of water on their voyage to Singapore.

7

Fighting the tide

Just after noon the spectacular volcanic form of Gunung (Mount) Agung on the northeast coast of Bali came into view, along with the island of Nusa Besar at the entrance to the dangerous Lombok Strait.

The 20-kilometre-wide, 60-kilometre-long passage between the islands of Bali and Lombok connects the Java Sea with the Indian Ocean and experiences some of the most powerful tidal rips on earth as the currents surge through the waterway.

Visibility was perfect, according to Lyon as Carse positioned the vessel so that she would transit the strait in the dark.

'Bearing due north magnetic,' Davidson wrote. 'These bearings confirm our dawn meridian fix. Speed still dead slow to get into position 20 miles [32 kilometres] south of Lombok by 1700 hours.'

At 4 pm Davidson noted, 'Must have been a helping set [following sea] as we have approached nearer than is prudent. Turned away to eastward for 20 minutes then back on our previous course again.'

An hour later, he wrote, 'Too near for any increase in speed. Maintained slow until sunset when full speed ahead with all our 6.3/4 knots for Lombok Strait.'

Lyon also noted that they set a course for the centre of the narrows at sunset, increasing the engine to the maximum revs. 'It soon became apparent that there was a considerable southerly set [opposing current] to contend with.'

For the MV *Krait*, with a maximum speed of just eight knots, a seven-knot tidal flow through the strait presented a significant navigational challenge given the Japanese outposts, the powerful searchlights located on both islands and the high numbers of enemy vessels and aircraft transiting the strait. Making just one knot of headway would mean that the boat would still be within the strait and in full view of enemy lookouts in broad daylight.

They first spotted an enemy searchlight at 7.20 pm. Davidson wrote, 'Powerful searchlight bearing red 80 illuminated sea in direct line with *Krait*. Light was below our horizon which is a bare four miles. Same light was burned at 19.30, 19.40, 19.55 and 20.35, with a single searching sweep. Considered to be a coast defence light on Bali.'

Horrie Young also noted, 'A searchlight pokes its slender beam out towards us, all hold our breaths, relief beam does not pick us up.'

They had planned to steam through the strait in the dead of night, but it was soon apparent that it was going to take much longer than expected as daylight and a favourable tide did not coincide.

Davidson wrote, 'First watch. Entered Lombok Strait where sea conditions were found to be confused. Many tide rips in an E–W direction, varying to NE–SW, mostly breaking in a fresh SE wind blowing into the strait. Passage was attempted on a course N.35 deg. E to pass between Nusa Besar and Lombok Is. From entry into strait until four hours later distance made good was under five miles at full speed. At times *Krait* was travelling backwards. Therefore the tidal current must have reached seven knots.'

At this stage the vessel was losing ground to the tide and it was only when the tide turned that she could make any headway.

Lyon meanwhile was recording detailed observations to add to the prodigious amount of intelligence they would be gathering during the voyage. This included any shipping activity and the location of shore-based facilities such as searchlights or enemy positions. 'Four hours were taken to pass the four-mile long island. Nusa Besar, under Dutch rule, was almost uninhabited except in the northwestern corner. It now seems to be the centre of some activity. Numerous controlled fires on the hillsides, indicating possible clearance of the bush, and both moving and fixed lights were observed.'

It was a frustrating night as they battled the ferocious tide. Carse recorded the tense time in his own log, another rare and valuable document which is held by the AWM: '0200: We commenced to make slight headway and by 0400 have made good six miles since midnight.'

But by dawn on 9 September their hope that the tide was now with them and would carry them through during the black of night had been dashed. 'Dawn showed us the fallacy of this hope,' noted Davidson. 'We woke to find ourselves right in the middle of the narrows between Bali and Lombok.'

They were like sitting ducks, completely exposed should the Japanese wonder about the little boat and decide to take a closer look. But whether it was their training or Lyon's and Davidson's skill in choosing the right personalities for the job, the crew went calmly about their duties despite the danger they found themselves in.

With Bali 11 nautical miles (20 kilometres) to port and Lombok nine nautical miles (17 kilometres) to starboard, Lyon wrote, 'The pilot [had] told us that during the East monsoon the peak of Bali was seldom visible, we therefore considered ourselves unlucky that, as the sun rose, every rock and tree on the volcano stood out very clearly in the conditions of almost perfect clearness. On the Lombok side we were luckier: a slight ground has prevented us from being seen at Ampenan, the only likely base in the area. Some small sailing craft were seen close inshore, but there was no sign of any patrol craft. This was the first opportunity to judge the crew under seemingly hazardous conditions. Their complete calm was most encouraging.'

It was not until 10 am that they were finally able to set a course for the southern coast of Borneo while staying clear of a number of local fishing vessels. This part of the journey would be extremely dangerous – something that all the men knew. On board the rickety boat, tension was running high.

'Anxious moment last night and this morning, ran into heavy current only making ¼ knot in spots,' wrote Young. 'Sighted Malayan prau about 11 am off starboard bow – first ship since we left. I'll bet he wouldn't be steaming so peacefully along two miles away if he knew our cargo and identity.'

All of the men felt the rising fear of being spotted out in the open seas. 'This war is certainly hard on the nervous system,' Carse noted in his log.

Moss Berryman has a vivid memory of the harrowing journey through the strait.

'When morning came, instead of being miles clear of Bali, which we were looking at all night, we could see their trucks moving around, the Japanese trucks moving around Bali. When morning came we were still in the middle of this Lombok Strait! We thought, this is going to be lovely. Somebody is going to come out and have a look at us,' he said.

Particularly nail-biting were those times when Japanese aircraft went overhead, with the pilots close enough to see. Berryman recalled that enemy seaplanes did take a close look at them on occasion and he clearly remembered waving to one Japanese pilot in his open cockpit who stuck his hand out and returned the greeting. But the rising sun flag atop the *Krait* had done its job and thankfully no Japanese plane returned for a second look.

The next week was spent steaming along the southern coast of Borneo towards the Lingga Islands that stretch along the north coast of Sumatra and about 100 kilometres southeast of Singapore.

Despite the strain of constant danger, Young still found time to marvel at the tropical marine and other wildlife – or perhaps it helped to take his mind off their perils. On 8 September, as they got into position to tackle the strait, he had spotted: 'Numerous large sharks seen during course of the day; one particularly large one endeavouring to knock large black sea-bird off floating log with its dorsal fin – no luck.'

On 9 September he noted: 'Sighted portion of Kangean Islands about supper time, also some beautiful coloured butterflies followed us for some miles. Lieut. Davidson caught one and identified it by some peculiar title. It had a very delicate perfume, possibly from some of its flowery haunts.'

Next day, he wrote, 'Plenty of flying fish. They prove to be very interesting – have examined a couple of specimens which came aboard during passage up the north east of Barrier Reef. They have two large fins which spread out just behind fish's head when flying and close into the back when in water.'

Young also made some close observations of the patterns of life as they motored through various island groups and many local fishing vessels. 'I can't help noticing how picturesque they look, typical of the East,' he mused.

What wasn't so pretty was the sight of the men painting themselves an even darker shade of brown as they approached their first objective on 15 September. 'God, if only my wife could see me now. Mr D took a photo – doubt will ever reach a publisher as no one has a stitch on – this dye is most uncomfortable but necessary for tomorrow we land in enemy territory. Incidentally we crossed the "line" [equator] about 7.30 am, no ceremony.'

It is traditional at sea for any vessel crossing the equator to conduct a 'crossing the line' ceremony where first timers are 'initiated' by King Neptune. Navy ships take this ancient practice very seriously and the ceremonies are often elaborate and at times inappropriate, but this was not the time or the place for risking such a display.

The planned staging point for the Jaywick raid was the island of Pompong at the southern end of the Riouw Archipelago, about 80 kilometres southeast of Singapore.

On 15 September the raiders experienced their first rainstorm of the voyage. About midnight the wind dropped and the sea became 'oily calm', according to Horrie Young's diary. He had never experienced anything quite like what followed.

'Approximately 1.30 am Sumatra [tropical storm] hit us with full force. Major Lyon recognised symptoms and immediately

79

ordered all hatches to be battened down and ship made ready for heavy weather. No sooner than he spoke, a peculiar sighing noise was heard and the works hit us. I sincerely hope I never witness another. The wind was terrific and I thought every moment the ship was going to be lifted bodily out of the water. The waves mounted and can well be imagined how we were treated – rain fell in torrents. It passed fairly quick (about three quarters of an hour) leaving a very disturbed area.'

These weather events, known as 'Sumatras' or squalls, are lines of thunderstorms that develop at night between March and November in the region. They are characterised by strong gusty winds and heavy rain that lasts an hour or two. It was a reminder that, so far, they had been extremely lucky with the weather in what was, after all, the southwest monsoon season.

Before daybreak, Davidson noted 'Middle watch. Slowed down to allow a large tanker to pass ahead on a northerly course. We were not sighted, or at least no apparent interest was taken in us. Ship seemed to be about 10,000 tons built on the latest lines.'

At 5.30 am on 16 September they passed between Sebank and Mesana islands, then moved up the Temiang Strait.

On entering the Lingga island group, approximately 100 kilometres from Singapore, Horrie Young wrote, 'Strange, all the lads engrossed in a bitter discussion on the English language and how it should be spoken.'

He was still full of wonder at his new surroundings: 'All around us are hundreds of islands also passed by some fine native sailing ships. Evidently busy in rich fishing trade around island group. They pass close – we may observe native crew at the job, also noticed many native villages on some of the larger groups.

'Very heavy vegetation on all – profuse in coconut palms. We gaze longingly but unsafe to land, our objective being Pompong

Island – a place of gruesome history, better it were named horror island, or finally may land at Temerang.' Pompong was to be the rear base for the raid on Singapore.

The island was the scene of the massacre of some 200 civilians, including British and Australian nurses fleeing Singapore on board the SS *Kuala* on 14 February 1942. The ship was bombed and sunk and survivors were machine gunned by Japanese aircraft.

As the vessel motored through the islands of the archipelago they had to remain clear of populated islands and local craft as Japanese aircraft continually passed overhead. The war was never far away as they passed numerous shipwrecks caused by enemy bombing.

'Sighted numbers of sailing craft,' noted Davidson. 'One was a European type sloop-rigged yacht of about 12 tons. Numbers of Bugis boats (undecked ketches, gaff rigged) and two- and three-masted junks. Proceeded to Pompong Is. to seek a hideout for *Krait*. Found nothing good, so tried Benku Is.'

That proved to be little better and they soon also realised that they needed to rethink their strategy for hiding the *Krait* while she waited to rendezvous with the canoeists.

Young wrote, 'Spent the afternoon cruising round looking for a suitable hide-out for *Krait* – unfortunately water too shallow and too many coral reefs.'

'Could not get into Benku bays and inlets on account of off-lying coral reefs,' wrote Davidson of their frustrating search for a safe secret hideaway for the *Krait*. 'All the islands in the vicinity are similar. So the alternative of going over to the Sumatra mangroves and river mouths was dropped. Instead it was decided that *Krait* should return to Borneo, and keep moving, after landing the operational party.'

Hiding in plain sight was a highly risky strategy, but they were left with little choice but to sneak around the coast of Borneo under cover of their old fishing boat and enemy flag.

At 2.25 pm a Japanese float plane came swooping along at about 2000 feet, Young wrote, 'No-one noticed until he was right on top of us. We all dived for cover trying to look as unconcernedly as possible – shock passes so does plane. I guess our flag did the trick. In the evening we notice searchlights in the middle of a group of islands. Led us to believe we are in the heart of an enemy seaplane base. We anchor as close inshore as possible and prepare to get operational party gear out and the mast comes down with a "crash".'

It was obvious by now that they were too close to a Japanese air base to establish a staging camp.

'There are a disturbing number of aircraft round here, all are flying low,' wrote Davidson at 4 pm on 16 September with his usual professional understatement. 'We had better try another area for our kick-off.'

They awoke next morning to the sounds of Japanese seaplanes flying right overhead and very low. 'No-one even dares to look at them,' wrote Horrie Young. 'Lookout states he heard aero engines warming up about 4 am. Sound carries for miles across these lagoons etc. About 8.30 am three natives in a canoe try to pay us a call but we anchor up and sail. I wonder what they think of our manners.'

Davidson wrote, 'All these indications, courses of float planes, revving of engines, playing of searchlights, point to presence of either an established seaplane base, not far from Chempa Is., Lingga Archipelago, or a warship lying there and carrying two different types of float-plane. The latter is unlikely. What a pity our commitments do not permit of our investigating and destroying the place.'

At 12.15 pm he noted, 'Identified Durian Is., the promised land of Stage II. Spent the day in preparing the operational party's gear for disembarkation tonight. Today will complete Stage I.'

Later that day Young wrote, 'Have been sailing in and out of the group all day waiting for night to put the party ashore – stage is all set. Many native villages and their fishing grounds sighted. We pass so close to one that we could see a large black dog with a white front walking up and down. The huts are built in the water on long sticks.'

After it became evident that Durian would not do due to its large population of locals, Lyon reported, 'It was planned to arrive at Durian, the original canoe hide, after dark, but the untimely arrival of the natives left us with a whole day in which to cover a distance of only 30 miles [48 kilometres]. To kill time we sailed north until close to the Petong group and then altered to East and approached Galang Bahru. When two miles from the shore we spotted a new building with an observation tower alongside it. Unchallenged, we cautiously altered course until heading as though bound from Sumatra to Singapore.

'North of Galang Bahru lies the island of Pandjang; as we passed along its western shore we noticed that there were some sandy coves and no signs of habitation. It seemed best that, having fully explored the local dangers, we should use this as our canoe base rather than risk unknown dangers around Durian.'

Lyon added, 'At nightfall *Krait* was in the entrance to the Bulan Strait and only 21 miles [34 kilometres] from Singapore, whose lights could be seen reflected in the clouds. Once certain that we could no longer be seen, we silenced our engine and headed back towards Pandjang. Almost immediately, a violent tropical storm swept down, obliterating all landmarks. Our navigation was greatly helped by the lights on the fishing pagars (inhabited fish traps), the positions of which we had noted on our way north.'

They reached Pandjang, which is close to the larger island of Rempang about 50 kilometres north of Pompong, about midnight.

Davidson noted, 'We anchored in three fathoms off a small beach about two-thirds of the way down from the north end. A strong wind had followed the storm and was blowing about Force Six from the southward, bringing with it a considerable swell and breaking seas, and beating against the flood tide. Breaking surf was all round the island making it impossible to land our valuable gear in our flat-bottomed dinghy.'

They looked around further but by the time they passed their original proposed landing beach on Pandjang Island again, the wind and sea had abated and it was thought good enough to attempt a landing there, according to Davidson's log. 'Anchored in five fathoms. A. B. Jones rowed Lieut. Davidson ashore to reconnoitre. The beach was found to be perfect, and landing conditions manageable with care.'

The men went ashore and found cover but no sign of habitation, according to Lyon. 'At dawn a more extensive recce revealed that there was a village about a quarter of a mile away on the island, but there was no sign of any track leading to our bay.'

After dark they returned and set about unloading all the operational gear and supplies, including food and water for one month. By 2.30 am three loads had been taken ashore when a junk passed the *Krait* on a northerly course, moving very slowly. Even though it was dark the vessel was still visible and sound carries clearly and a long way across open water.

'Landing activities were delayed meanwhile. Eventually all the operational party and its gear were ashore by 03.45, and

84

A. B. Berryman rowed the dinghy back to *Krait*, who sailed silently away to the SE,' wrote Davidson.

Or, as Horrie Young put it, '1 am – the canoeists are landing with their equipment – heavy swell running and we stand in about 50 yards off island beach – appears to be uninhabited, we sincerely hope so. Four-thirty am landing successful. We weigh anchor and go for our lives to Borneo coast.'

Lyon was the last to leave the *Krait* and Young clearly recalled him saying to Carse, 'Now remember, Ted, if we are not back by the rendezvous date you are to take *Krait* back to Australia.'

'It was quite an emotional moment,' Young said. 'I think most of us had doubts as to whether we would ever see our colleagues again, such was the almost impossible nature of their mission.'

As Carse turned the vessel towards Temiang Strait and the China Sea, he wondered why his irritated eyes were stinging and he realised that he was crying because he felt that he would never see the men again.

8

Hiding in plain sight

The *Krait* weighed anchor at 4.30 am on 18 September with her depleted crew of eight men. She was bound for the islands and inlets along the south coast of Borneo where she would spend the next fortnight trying to dodge enemy patrols and nosy locals while maintaining her cover of an authentic Japanese fishing boat simply going about her business.

She would then return, sailing back to reach their designated rendezvous point on the island of Pompong in time to collect the raiders, who faced an 80-kilometre paddle through the chain of islands following their mission, before setting a course for home. At least, that was the plan.

Before dawn had broken the *Krait* had run the gauntlet of some powerful searchlights and four Japanese aircraft but by 8 am had 'shaken off our islands', as Horrie Young put it in his diary, leaving the Riouw Archipelago behind.

As the *Krait* motored southeast towards the south coast of Borneo the weight of responsibility was all on Carse's shoulders. He was the only remaining officer with a motley crew of eight – who hardly constituted a cutting-edge commando raiding party –with the mission to evade capture and return to collect the six canoeists, whose lives would largely depend on the *Krait* making the rendezvous. He was also the only one with the skill to navigate the *Krait* successfully back to Pompong and take them all home again.

As Young wrote later in his memoir: 'To properly gauge the seriousness of Carse's position we should consider the composition of his reduced ship's company which now comprised one mid-aged Leading Stoker [McDowell] who was fully engaged in nursing *Krait*'s ailing propulsion system, one Leading Telegraphist [Young] who was a communications specialist possessed of the minimal firearm experience and weapons training that goes with that branch of the service, a Medical Orderly [Morris] who under the Geneva Accord is not permitted to carry firearms and three seaman branch personnel [Berryman, Marsh and Cain] who, although possessing a significant amount of training in the use of firearms, had not the battle-hardened experience of say an 8th Army veteran. We also had our cook [Crilly] who notwithstanding his mustering as a transport motor mechanic would have had experience in the use of firearms but was not in particularly good health and was about to be retired from active service.'

Finally, there was Carse himself – 'a man of middle-age and also in very indifferent health; I am quite sure we younger people really had no comprehension of the gravity of our position'.

Young wrote on 19 September that after landing the party of canoeists in the dead of night everyone had been 'dog-tired' and that the remaining eight crewmen were having to work pretty hard. 'My principal job now is to monitor all Jap transmissions so we may learn if our boys have been captured. The 24th is going to be Guy Fawkes night — we will hug the radio from then on. Curious to know what the Japs will have to say.'

Presciently, he also speculated that the enemy would probably say it had been internal sabotage 'and shoot a couple of hundred Chinks'.

Plying further into enemy-held waters the tension on board was building as Carse noted in his logbook: 'Our present job reminds me very much of the anxious father waiting outside the maternity ward for news. The only difference is that his worries and anxiety pass, as a rule, with the arrival of the triplets in a few hours or so while ours is to drag on for a fortnight and when the time does come we expect a lusty, overgrown family of six.'

By all accounts the crusty Carse was not given to outbursts of spontaneous praise but he made his feelings very clear regarding the efforts of the ship's engineer, Paddy McDowell, 'He has worked day and night training crew and operatives to help him in his duties and to be able to operate the engine should anything happen to him, as well as tending and servicing the engine. In fact, he looks after the engine better and treats it more carefully than a mother would a baby. No matter how long the hours he works away, stopping troubles before they have developed and always cheerful and happy. No man could be better suited to the job than he is.'

Moss Berryman regarded the World War I Royal Navy submarine service veteran as an almost mystical figure. Berryman and Fred Marsh, the young bucks of the crew, were assigned as assistant engineers and had to learn how to operate the machinery in case anything should happen to their more experienced shipmate.

'If he kicked the bucket while we were away, well, Freddy and I knew how to stop and start it,' Berryman said.

McDowell was a real character, he added, and he remembered that sometimes when they were relaxing on deck, Paddy would tell one of them to 'get a tin'.

'We had a few tins of peaches or apricots and we used to save the tins. If you were told to "get a tin" you would go down and fill it up with oil from a certain tap on the engine. Paddy would get a mouthful of the oil and he'd announce, "There's bloody water getting in somewhere", he'd pick it. When we asked him how he did it he would say, "You learned a lot in those first submarines, they broke down all the time".'

During the next few days Young's diary is brief but to the point. On 20 September he reported that they had passed a Chinese junk about four miles (six kilometres) abeam. 'Nothing much of interest today. No news of the boys and no enemy planes sighted.'

Carse noted, 'Our bottom is getting very dirty. Long green weeds about four inches [10 centimetres] long all round so we will have to run to Borneo and put in a day or so scraping. As we don't pick up the party till the 1st, we have plenty of time. I hope they are finding it as easy as we are and they have a successful trip. We are looking forward to seeing them again.'

The next day, 21 September, Young wrote: 'Passed large group of islands late in the afternoon – heavy seas running. Some of the group, according to Dutch report, are inhabited so we sail ever onwards.'

Carse, meanwhile, was dwelling on the skills of his crew. 'Our cook is certainly living up to his name of Pancake Andy. We get them at least once a day. When the cruise commenced, pancakes were one of my favourites. At the present rate if I ever look at one again I will be sick. I must admit however that they are far more appetising than hard biscuits. What wouldn't we give for a loaf of bread and a good sirloin steak. When the cook was engaged for the trip he was in the sappers. His cooking qualifications were that he was a fair motor mechanic and had a rough idea how to cook pancakes. He has. On the whole he has done an excellent job.

'Acting Leading Seaman Cain is also another excellent hand capable in all branches of seamanship, willing to work at any time and for any length of time and always cheerful.'

But as always they were desperate to know how the raiders were getting on. 'The Japanese news broadcasts are now our main delight. We listen to hear if there is any news of our party – of which no news is good news.'

At 7 pm he logged that they were passing between Buan and Pelapsis islands. They were having an unusual but welcome day of respite from snooping planes or boats.

'No ship or humans sighted all day. This seems like paradise but I suppose that tomorrow will bring at least sailing ships.'

He was right. The next day, 22 September, Young reported that they had sighted a large sailing vessel off to port. 'We alter course as intelligence reports say Jap is using similar types for island patrols. No incident all day, seas getting worse.'

This was two days before the designated raid on Singapore harbour. For the *Krait* still at sea, the weather worsened. 'Had to turn and run before sea as things a little dangerous,' wrote Young. 'Going half-speed. Wireless reports indicated things not going too well for Axis – after tomorrow night things will be going a lot less well, for the Nips in particular.'

Carse reported, 'Since we dropped the party we have had to reorganise our watch keeping bill. Leading Telegraphist Young is now a watch keeper, getting time off to listen into Japanese and British news programs and the cook is training as Quartermaster in his spare time.'

Then it was back to the topic of food. '1600 hours: our cook is experimenting. Today he made what was quite a good resemblance of a steam pudding. So close a resemblance, in fact, that the crew have specifically requested that instead of a sample like today he puts on a meal of it tomorrow.

'So far since we left the party I have been able to run by dead reckoning [location based on last known position, speed, course and elapsed time] and by careful treatment my eyes are becoming better. I hope they are all right for our final flutter homeward.'

The next day, 24 September, Carse noted, 'This waiting about is the worst part of the trip so far. Well, the show is on tonight and that completes half our estimate in Japanese waters. After that it remains to pick them up and return home. If the trip is a success we are thinking of renaming *Krait* "The Singapore Terror". Seems more appropriate.'

But the same day, the remaining crew on board the *Krait* soon had plenty to think about other than the raid, when she narrowly avoided becoming a shipwreck.

'KFM [*Krait*] nearly went to the port of missing ships – nearly mistook the coast of Borneo for low lying cloud,' Young reported. 'Finished up only 200 yards [180 metres] from the shore. Struck bottom three times, finally had to anchor and did we get a pasting. *KFM* [*Krait*] rolled dangerously all night – nobody had any sleep – gale blew all day – had to turn around and run before it nearly all day. Cleared large group of islands off Borneo coast.'

As the mission progressed rations were being carefully monitored and Young noted that his lunch on 25 September was a handful of raisins, half a cup of water and one biscuit. 'Will certainly make up for lost time when I get back.'

Thinking about food was one way to distract themselves from worrying about the fate of the six canoeists who were supposed to have carried out their mission the night before. The minutes passed with agonising slowness as they waited for news.

That day Carse, with considerable understatement, wrote, 'Well, we are waiting for the first Japanese broadcast now to tell us news of Singapore. Let's hope it has the honourable Jap running around in circles for a few days. This waiting for something to happen is not easy and news of the raid would be very welcome. Not only would it assure us of the welfare of the party but would indicate that our main object had been achieved. The trip according to schedule has now entered its second part and everyone on board is pining for land. It is now 23 days since we have set foot on land and the space at our disposal is very limited for exercise so we feel it more than on a big ship. If everything runs to schedule we should clear Lombok Strait on the night of the ninth of October.'

It is evident that the lack of news was starting to get to the men, who did not know whether the raiders had been successful or whether the *Krait* would be sailing back into the arms of a Japanese reception party at Pompong Island.

At midday on 26 September, Carse wrote, 'So far no news has come over the wireless about Singapore. All they seem to be doing is to try and impress the civilian population with the vast superiority of the Imperial Japanese Air Force and the vast amount of men that will be needed to take their gains off them. They have so far made no mention of Lae, Salamaua or Finschhafen [which the Allies had by then recaptured from the Japanese in New Guinea] so it seems they are nearing the end of their tether and just trying to get the Allies to cry off the war and give them time to build up for another go at world dominance.'

On a more humorous note, he added: 'As the only clothes worn nowadays are sarongs, we will probably be forgetting when we get back to civilisation and all be arrested for indecent exposure.'

On the same day, according to Young's log, they sighted a suspicious vessel that, on seeing the *Krait*, altered course towards her.

'Skipper thought it may be a Jap patrol vessel as intelligence reports say the Nips are using several such types – two cases of pineapples [hand grenades], Owen guns and other machine guns made ready in case. I'd reckon he'd get a hell of a surprise – we could dispose of him all nice and quiet as we are just out of sight of the Borneo coast (10 miles [16 kilmetres]),' Young recorded. Fortunately the boat turned away and confrontation was avoided.

The shortage of fresh water remained a constant problem on this leg of the voyage – as it did throughout the mission – and every downpour of rain was greeted with a throng of empty containers and naked bodies as the men sought relief from filth and the tropical heat.

Young added, also on 26 September, that the weather had been extremely calm. 'It rained last night – thank God. Am having a little trouble making water ration spin out owing to excessive heat – you can't walk on wooden decks. My behind is severely sunburnt so much so I can't sit down which is most uncomfortable – the rest of my body is nearly the colour of a native I have browned so.'

Young was almost constantly monitoring his radio after 24 September for news of the raid, but with no result.

'Real *Krait* weather, beautiful and calm so we stopped in middle of Java Sea and proceeded to scrape the sides and did a spot of fishing,' he wrote on 27 September. 'So far Tokyo radio hasn't mentioned our raid on Singapore.'

Carse noted, 'It seems peculiar that we should be drifting round the China Sea with men working in a dinghy alongside scraping the bottom on a beautiful day just as if Mr Tojo had not been heard of. Yesterday Leading Telegraphist Young picked up what appeared to be a recall signal to a flight of nine planes. They seemed close to him but we didn't see them. I think this means that we would be safer to keep underway during daylight hours anyways. It might also mean that they have caught our party or abandoned the search. We should know which on the first when we make the rendezvous.'

Despite their constant anxiety about the raiding party, Young described 28 September as one of the best days of the trip. 'It rained this morning and everyone rushed out in birthday suits, even the skipper, for a lovely shower. It was worth more than a fiver. We put everything capable of holding water out to catch a few precious drops, water is more precious than gold to us – it is the key to our very existence. The sea is very calm but the sky is still very overcast.

'Tonight at midnight we turn about and dash full speed to Singapore, pick up the lads and full speed for home – God it will be grand to see Aussie again and get a decent feed.'

Carse noted, 'It is lovely to feel clean even if it is only for a few hours as tomorrow we will have to blacken up again for our run across to the Lingga Islands and up Temiang Strait.'

Yet despite their extraordinarily tense circumstances, morale on the *Krait* did not plummet as she prepared to turn towards the island of Pompong. The trusty boat and her motley crew had successfully completed another part of the mission, and hope and anticipation drove them onwards.

Moss Berryman was comforted throughout this tense period by the words of Ivan Lyon and even 74 years later he clearly recalled what his commander had said: 'Don't think this is dangerous; it is quite an adventure.'

'He would say things like that to take our minds off things,' Berryman said.

With 29 September the turning point in the voyage, Young noted, 'On our way home via Singapore. Unfortunately, we have to get blackened up again tomorrow which is most uncomfortable but a necessity. We are to attempt to break into his [the Japanese] front door and rescue our canoeists. Time will tell if we are successful. So far Japan has not mentioned a thing about the raid on the wireless so we don't know whether our boys have been captured and we may be sailing into a well-prepared trap however we will be prepared for emergencies.

'At present sitting on top of the wireless equipment is enough plastic explosive to blow half of Sydney up so the ship will be blown up and we take to the bush to sell our lives at the best possible price as no-one cares to be taken prisoner, the Nips are much too generous.'

At 9.40 am he added, 'Several islands are on either side of us. Native fishermen are proceeding about their normal duties while we sail in and out amongst them – makes me feel like the wolf in sheep's clothing.'

On 29 September Carse wrote, 'At 1500 we had 292 miles to cover to get to the entrance to Temiang and 47 hours to do it in. This should give us a slight margin.'

The next day, 30 September, Carse noted, 'Another day gone. Tomorrow night we should know our fate for if we make contact safely the job is almost done.'

After a fortnight in the close company of the young men a reflective Carse added: 'In future operations it would be better if the crew were older than say 25. The younger members do not seem to realise their responsibilities as they should and have to be told continuously to do their ordinary routine duties. A fight with a patrol boat would not find them wanting but might prove fatal to the result of the cruise. If this trip is a success we can honestly say that the Japanese contributed greatly to it. As we have to use Japanese pencils, Japanese sun glasses and drawing pins, all of these are essential so we have something to thank them for.'

On a pragmatic note Young recorded: 'Last day of the month – Navy owes me eight pounds eight shillings. It will come in very handy when I get back. Nothing much of interest sighted, still steaming west nor west.'

9

Into the jaws of the lion

While the *Krait* was sailing away from Pandjang Island before dawn on 18 September with a depleted crew, the six raiders set about establishing their first hide as they prepared for the marathon mission that lay ahead of them – paddling by night and hiding by day.

As daylight broke, they saw a family of otters playing in pools on the water's edge, so they christened their new rear base 'Otter Bay'.

'We carried our stores about twenty-five yards [23 metres] back into the jungle and pitched our tents beside a water hole,' reported Lyon, according to the Naval Board report. 'By noon we had hidden our reserves of food in a cliff face and on returning to the camp were pleased to find that an army of hermit crabs had obliterated our tracks on the beach. We kept a sentry posted in an OP [observation post], who reported the usual activity of small junks and fishing craft. Transport aircraft were also observed in a north and south course. These were a daily occurrence throughout the operation; it later transpired that they left Kallang aerodrome in the early morning for the south and arrived from the south about noon. Between five and ten of these aircraft passed overhead daily and soon ceased to interest us.'

After Davidson conducted his reconnoitre of the island and returned to announce that there was a small kampong (village) about 400 metres away, he found that his comrades had discovered a freshwater spring where they could enjoy a bath as well as safe drinking water.

They were exhausted after a day of hard labour and after 40 days at sea since leaving Cairns their physical condition had softened and they were somewhat out of shape.

Lyon noted, 'Having been landed on the base ahead of schedule, it was possible to use the 18th and 19th September as rest days. On the 20th we spent the day checking over our stores and equipment in preparation for starting at dusk.'

While they slept, one sentry always remained on duty to keep an eye on the passing parade of enemy patrol boats, local fishermen and the stream of Japanese planes flying in and out of Singapore.

Davidson, who was now in command as attack leader and was ever the hard taskmaster, insisted on a regular routine of physical exercise to rebuild the canoeists' sagging muscles for the long, hard paddle ahead.

On 20 September the three two-man teams of Lyon and Huston, Davidson and Falls, and Page and Jones unpacked and assembled their 5.2-metre folding canvas-covered canoes. Each vessel would carry more than 300 kilograms of weight, including the two operatives, food for a week, six tins of canned heat,

10 litres of water, various tablets including medicine, water purifying and energy, two jungle parangs, binoculars, mosquito nets and groundsheets as well as three sets of three limpet mines plus a spare, detonators, primer cord, magnetic holdfasts and a short broomstick which would be used to apply the mines beneath the waterline and out of sight. Each canoe also carried a small silk sail and collapsible mast. The food was stowed in the stern with water and explosives in the forward compartment.

Over their khaki shorts each raider wore a two-piece suit of waterproof (non-breathable) black japara silk, two pairs of black cotton socks, black sandshoes with strengthened soles and a black webbing belt fitted with .38 revolver and 100 rounds, sheath knife and short rubber hose loaded with lead. Davidson also wore his faithful throwing stiletto. In zip pockets were a compass and a first-aid kit that included morphine syringes. When they were ready to go, Lyon produced a small tin containing the cyanide pills that he promised would take effect in five seconds and that he would issue to each man prior to the attack.

Under the cover of darkness, after scouring the campsite for any telltale trace of their presence, the six black-faced raiders boarded their canoes and disappeared silently into the sea, their sharp-edged paddles barely raising a whisper.

Lyon noted, 'Our departure was slightly delayed by the passage of a 70 foot [21-metre] patrol launch, a mile to seaward of the bay. The noise of her exhaust had been heard at regular intervals on the two previous nights; we were not, therefore, worried by her presence.

'The canoes, when loaded with food and water for a week, operational stores and men, a total cargo of approximately 700 lbs [317 kilograms], were very low in the water and sluggish. We paddled out into deep water and carried out our normal routine of sinking all debris, such as tins, that might betray our presence.'

With Davidson and Falls in the lead, they continued paddling away from Otter Bay in a tight arrowhead formation and headed northwest along the coast of Rempang Island. After five and a half hours and about 18 kilometres the dog-tired canoeists pulled into the tiny Pulau Bulat ('Pulau' means 'island' in Malay) after midnight. The waters around Singapore Island are dotted with many such minute islands.

'On recce it proved to be a small uninhabited [knoll] with a sandy beach,' Lyon wrote in his journal. 'Here we spent a pleasant day observing the passage of numerous small craft in and out of the strait, under conditions of such safety that it was possible to allow bathing.'

As the men took a dip in the sea to relieve themselves of the stench generated by their silk suits Davidson, who was also the mission's official photographer, took a snap of his smiling colleagues with another island and native village in the background.

The image captures the five operatives looking more like holidaymakers than special forces raiders hiding far behind enemy lines and engaged in one of the most daring and dangerous commando missions ever undertaken.

At dusk they continued up the strait but owing to constant false alarms the canoes made poor progress. The strait was a nightmare as the tides and current played havoc with the heavily laden folboats. Lyon and Huston had particular trouble and at times could not control their craft. Lyon was physically the weakest of the six paddlers and had missed many of the tough training sessions back in Cairns.

Lyon wrote, 'After making good only twelve miles [19 kilometres] were obliged to shelter in a sand fly infested swamp to avoid being caught out in daylight. The hide was a bad one; throughout the day small boats passed us and we were exactly opposite a village on the island of Boyan, 300 yards [275 metres] away. At dusk we were still undetected and had learnt from our miserable day the important lessons that ample time must be allowed for a recce before a hide is selected.'

On the evening of 22 September, however, they made excellent progress. 'By 2030 hours we had reached the end of the strait and could see ahead of us the lights of Pulau Sambu, formerly a Dutch oil depot, five miles [eight kilometres] south of Singapore,' Lyon wrote.

He and Davidson had chosen the fateful island of Dongas, which lay just 12 kilometres from Singapore, as their forward observation post and attack base.

'We arrived off it without incident at midnight on 22/23 September,' he wrote. 'A careful recce revealed that it was a jungle-covered hump of land, with an extensive swamp on the south side. It was uninhabited and had only one landing place, a narrow inlet in the swamp with a sandy cover at its head. Here a sand spit ran back into the swamp providing every facility for concealment with some comfort. We further explored the island in daylight and found that the high ground on the north side provided an excellent view of the Roads. Drinking water was found in a disused well. The island, therefore, fulfilled our requirements. By this time all members of the party were feeling the effects of their exertions, so the 23rd September was largely devoted to rest.'

The date 23 September had brought their 'adventure' to a total of 21 days and 3200 kilometres since they had left Exmouth; 45 days after departing from Cairns and just one day before their designated date for attacking the fortress of Singapore, the 'city of the lion'.

Through their powerful telescopes and binoculars they kept a night watch until 11 pm. Their watch revealed no sign of any defensive activity on the part of the Japanese occupiers, according to Lyon, who noted that in conditions of good visibility they could see right into Keppel Harbour and the many ships at anchor.

'There was no blackout in Singapore and the lights of cars driving down Beach Road could clearly be seen. No harbour or navigation lights were burning and all shipping was stationary,' he wrote.

When 24 September, the date designated for the attack, dawned they were all well rested and continued to maintain a keen watch, carefully scrutinising the details of both shore and shipping in the city that Lyon knew like the back of his hand – and which also held 12,000 Allied prisoners in inhumane conditions at the infamous Changi prison on the eastern tip of the island.

'There was no change to be seen in the general outline of the city,' Lyon wrote. 'A row of five to seven tall wireless masts have been constructed on the site of the former Paya Labar Station and there is a single mast on the roof of the Cathay Building. On the southernmost point of St John's Island there is now a small signal station. At Sambu, three miles from our OP, all visible oil tanks were still as left by the Dutch. There was tremendous activity on the western side of the island: the hammering of plates and drone of engines by day and night suggested either ship repair or building.'

As for their target, the shipping, there was considerable movement of vessels both in the harbour and Roads.

'At no time during the five days of observation was there less than 100,000 tons at the same time,' he wrote. 'Ships arrived from the east, either singly or in groups – none of these exceeded five ships and only one group was escorted. All were heavily laden and proceeded direct to their anchorage. Those ships seen to leave again for the east were, in many cases, lightly laden or in ballast. The point of departure for ships entering the Malacca Strait was obscured from Dongas; it is not, therefore, possible to judge the quantity of shipping leaving for the west.'

There was also some excellent news for the canoeists. 'Absence of patrol vessels and freedom of movement by medium-draught native craft convinced us that there were no minefields in the harbour.'

By late in the afternoon of 24 September, Lyon said, they had observed a total of 65,000 tons of shipping assembling in the Roads opposite Dongas. In modern military parlance this represented a 'target-rich environment' – but not an easy one.

'It was realised,' he wrote, 'that unfavourable tides would render an attack on this shipping difficult, but the nature of the target was such that an attempt seemed imperative.'

Unable to resist having a go, all three canoes set off at 8 pm and proceeded to paddle towards the target area.

'No patrols were encountered or enemy activity noted until midnight, when a weak searchlight on a high building in Singapore [probably the Cathay] was exposed in the direction of the canoes, for a period of about half a minute,' Lyon's journal noted.

But at 1 am, finding it impossible to make any progress against the strong tide, they were forced to abandon the attack.

Canoes 2 (Davidson and Falls) and 3 (Page and Jones) made it back to the hide on Dongas before daylight but the weakest pair, Canoe 1 (Lyon and Huston) were forced to hide among some boulders at the shore in order to avoid being spotted by locals at dawn.

According to the Navy Board report: 'This party spent an unhappy day sitting in the rain, only finding out when darkness permitted freedom of movement that they had landed on the south coast of Dongas. 'No 1 canoe rejoined the main party at 1900 hours. Lieutenant Davidson had anticipated their arrival and organised a much-needed hot meal; he had also made plans for an immediate change to an alternative hide, whence an attack could be launched the following night, 26/27, under favourable conditions. His prompt action on this occasion contributed greatly to the success of the expedition.'

So the next night, 25 September, the entire party moved past Sambu, arriving shortly before dawn at a small bracken-covered island called Subar that overlooked the harbour's Examination Anchorage.

'This OP has no beach and is waterless,' Lyon noted, 'but it provides an excellent vantage point from which to observe activities in Singapore, However, as all members of the expedition were in need of sleep, observation was limited.'

Nevertheless, in the late afternoon they were able to detail specific targets for each of the pairs of raiders. Davidson and Falls (Canoe 2) would hit ships in Keppel Harbour; Lyon and Huston (Canoe 1) would paddle to shipping moored at Examination Anchorage and Page and Jones (Canoe 3) would attack vessels at the wharves on the small island of Bukum.

An exhausted Ivan Lyon suggested that, because of the delays, after the attack the fastest canoe – Davidson and Falls – should bypass the canoeists' planned rendezvous on Dongas Island and head straight for Pompong and the scheduled assignation with the *Krait* at midnight on 1 October, to hold her there while the other two canoes caught up as quickly as they could. Davidson agreed and as the sun set over the warm tropical sea the raiders settled in for their last supper together.

As dusk approached they carried the limpet mines and water tins to the beach, before lumping the heavy canoes down from their hiding place for the beginning of the final phase of their epic mission. By 7 pm all the canoes were loaded and the excited raiders bid each other good luck.

* * *

Davidson and Falls (Canoe 2), who had the furthest to travel, immediately set off for Keppel Harbour.

'The flood tide was on the starboard, making progress slow,' Davidson's report stated, 'but even so we reached the passage by 2115 hours. The approach was uneventful with the exception of a searchlight on Blakang Mati, which searched the sky every now and then. Heavy tide rips enable us to keep to the water boat channel and soon the pylons of Keppel Harbour boom were visible.'

However, disaster nearly struck the canoe. 'A big steam ferry, a tug, burning navigation lights, and bound to the south of Blakang Mati, nearly ran us down, but we were not sighted,' Davidson wrote.

Clearing the ferry, their fortunes turned for the better when they discovered that the boom gate at the Tanjong Pagar end was open with no boom vessel in attendance. So they sneaked through and set about identifying the best targets.

'Inside the boom against the east wharf were two ships but they were too small to be worthy of attack. No shipping was seen at the main wharf, and that in the Empire Docks was too brilliantly lit up and too small to warrant attack.'

Fortunately for them, the boom gate was still unattended.

'We turned back and crossed over the boom again, heading for the Roads. Here there were many excellent targets and we selected three of the largest cargo vessels.'

Target number 1 was a 5000–6000-ton cargo vessel, heavily laden but they could not identify her name. 'Unfortunately her description fitted in with 15 Japanese ships.'

Target number 2 was again a 5000–6000-ton cargo vessel, with her engines aft and heavily laden. 'This was identified as the *Taisyo Maru* which had been seen on the Roads on 24th September,' Davidson noted.

Target number 3 was a similar vessel but evidently empty, and did not resemble any Japanese ship that they had on their list.

They paddled in close to the port side of each vessel away from Singapore's lights. In the relative darkness they attached the limpet mines below the waterline at about 10 pm. All the timers on the three canoes had been set to explode the mines at 5 am next morning.

'We timed ourselves by a chiming clock (probably on Victoria Hall) that told us quarter hours.'

With a great sense of relief tinged with exhaustion they paddled hell for leather to get out of there safely, heading off on a difficult, island-hopping journey to make the rendezvous with *Krait*.

'At 0115 hour on 27th September we left the Roads and headed for the Riouw Straits,' Davidson would report. 'We halted at a point of land six miles [10 kilometres] west of Pulau Nonosa and left again at 1900 hours proceeding in the direction of Pulau Tanjong Sau. Here we landed shortly before 0430 hours on 28th and left again at 1900 hours, passing to the north of Pulau Lepang to Tanjohg Piau, thence to Pulau Anak Mati and down the channel between Pulau Rempang and Pulau Sepokeo. Off Tanjong Klinokino we encountered the patrol boat and had to hug the bay.'

They had barely made it back to their base at Otter Bay on Pandjang Island early on 29 September, the day before the rendezvous date, when a fierce storm erupted. They were planning a risky daylight paddle to keep their rendezvous but due to the weather they instead spent the day resting until they set off at 7 pm for their final lap to link up with the *Krait*.

But once again the weather turned against them. 'When four miles [six kilometres] from Pulau Abang Besar a violent storm arose, bringing with it a deluge of rain, thunder and lightning, and lashing the sea into a fury,' Davidson wrote. 'We kept the bows of the canoe into the wind and sea and were tossed about for two hours, when the storm abated. We landed on Abang Besar and left again at 1900 hours on 30th September.

'Pulau Pompong, our rendezvous with *Krait*, was reached at 0100 hours 1st October. *Krait* appeared at 0015 on the morning of the 2nd October.'

* * *

The other two canoes – Page and Jones (Canoe 3) and Lyon and Huston (Canoe 1) – set off together at 7.20 pm on 26 September, 20 minutes after Davidson and Falls.

'Headed for the lights of Singapore between Pulau Skbarok and St John's Island,' wrote Page in his report. 'Paddling was easy, the tide being on our starboard quarter. The canoes kept together until about 2130, when they separated for their respective target areas.'

By 10.20 pm Page and Jones had reached their first target, namely the wharves at Pulau Bukum.

'The whole length of the wharves was examined and only one suitable target found alongside,' he reported later. 'This was an old freighter type, later identified as possibly of the Tone Maru class. A large tanker and a nondescript "engines aft" vessel were tied up at the wharves, but the former was both too big and fully laden and the latter was too small, to warrant attack.'

The wharves were lit normally. 'Arabic numerals were in use in numbering them, and a sentry was on guard near the bows of the tanker, stationed on the wharf. A large barge with arc lights was also alongside, on which many shadowy figures were working amongst what appeared to be cauldrons of steam. The exact nature of this work could not be defined.'

By 11 pm the tide had turned and was now running west to east. They cut silently through the water up to their first target – the Tone Maru–class freighter – and attacked it from the stern, attaching their limpet mines below the waterline. Leaving alone the other two vessels that they had already discounted as not being suitable, they made their way towards Keppel Harbour and their second target.

'This was a modern freighter with engine aft; three sets of goalpost masts. It was later identified as the *Nasusan Maru*,' wrote Page. They placed their charges on this vessel and continued on towards their third target, another freighter, which they attacked from midships aft.

'This was identified later as either the *Yamataga Maru* or the *Nagano Maru*,' wrote Page.

Then they too got out of there as fast as they could. 'The tide was still on the starboard quarter on the way back to Pulau Sambu. Pulau Sambu was brilliantly lit up and seemed to be at work even at that time of the morning. From Pulau Sambu to Pulau Dongas was a paddle against the tide, but we reached Dongas half an hour before the first explosion.'

As for Canoe 1 (Lyon and Huston), Lyon wrote 'Page and I decided to remain together during the approach to the target area. We paddled at an easy pace, making good progress on the cross tide, only pausing when the Blakang Mati searchlights shone uncomfortably close to us. By 2130 we had reached the vicinity of Pulau Jong, where we parted company.'

He and Huston did not have as much luck identifying targets as the other two pairs of canoeists and their target area was close to the ships attacked by Page and Jones.

'I arrived in my target area about 2230 to find that all shipping, except tankers, were blacked out and completely invisible against the background of hills. After some searching I located a ship, but on close inspection found that it "belonged to Page". When my time limit was exhausted I decided to attack a tanker, two of which I could clearly distinguish by the red light in place of the normal white anchor light. We made a direct approach from astern and placed two limpets on the engine room and one on the propeller shaft.'

But they were to have a shockingly narrow escape.

'Halfway through the work, Huston drew my attention to a man who was watching us intently from a porthole ten feet above. He continued to gaze until just before we left the ship when he withdrew his head and lighted his bedside lamp. He took no apparent action and we set off for Dongas 12 miles away.'

They reached it just before Page and Jones. 'We arrived at 0515 just as the first explosion occurred in the Examination Anchorage. Page and Jones arrived a few moments later. Dawn was breaking and the natives had been roused by the activity in the harbour. We therefore lost no time in gaining the shelter of the mangroves, from which we could observe any unusual activity around our Dongas hide.

'At 1100 we decided that it would be safe to make the crossing and we returned to our old campsite. Davidson meanwhile had decided to return to Pompong by way of the Riouw Strait and had found a hide some distance down the coast of Batam.'

10

The day that shook
the enemy

The explosions started just before daylight. Lyon, Huston, Page and Jones, who had holed up within sight and earshot of the harbour, were able to witness for themselves some of the colossal damage they had inflicted on the enemy. The men were exhilarated by what they saw as their handiwork sank or damaged enemy ships across the 'impregnable' harbour.

In all, seven explosions were heard between 5.15 am and 5.50 am, according to *The Official History of Special Operations Australia* (Volume 2): 'As the sun rose the Examination Anchorage could be clearly observed. One ship seen sunk by the stern with her bows protruding from the water. A tanker was burning fiercely and belching forth thick black smoke, which almost entirely covered the area. Owing to the haze and the smoke no other results could be seen. Fifteen minutes after the first explosion, ship sirens started and after another 15 minutes Singapore and Sambu were blacked out.'

The Naval Board official report summarised the 'observed results' of this historic mission in typical unemotional, military operational language:

'No 1 Canoe – Major Lyon, AB Huston. Failed to locate blacked out targets in the area south of Pasir Panjang: on return journey attacked the tanker *Sinkoku Maru* 10,020 tons in the Examination Anchorage.

'Observed results: The explosion of the limpets was followed by a large oil fire. At 1600 hours the vessel was observed to be down by the stern and smoking.

'No 2 Canoe – Lieut Davidson, AB Falls. Entered Keppel Harbour through the open Boom but failed to locate a suitable target in the Tanjong Pagar and East Wing Area. Subsequently attacked three freighters averaging 5000 tons in the West End of Singapore Roads.

'Observed results: Three explosions were heard in the Roads between 0545 and 0600. During the afternoon there was considerable activity of harbour craft in this area.

'No 3 Canoe – Lieut Page, AB Jones. Attacked one [freighter] alongside Bukum Wharf. A similar ship in Bukum Roads and a third engine aft type, in the Examination Anchorage. Possible average 4000 tons.

'Observed results: Three explosions were heard and in the afternoon the ship attacked in the Bukum Roads was seen to have sunk by the stern with her fore part still above the surface.'

The operatives estimated that they had sunk or badly damaged seven enemy ships for a total estimated tonnage of about 37,000. That was later downgraded to about 26,000 tonnes, but that was still more than was sunk by any single RAN warship during the entire war. The raid was a triumph, but the canoeists were too exhausted after paddling some 80 kilometres around Singapore waters in just 60 hours to savour the moment.

At dawn some of the ships in the harbour were seen to be under weigh, cruising aimlessly about.

'The sirens and noise continued most of the morning of the 27 September. After things had quietened down a bit there was considerable activity of small harbour craft in the target areas, and motor launches patrolled the north coast of Batam Island,' the Naval Board report said.

The first planes seen to take off came from Kallang at about 6.15 am and flew out towards the Malacca Straits, evidently to search for the cause of the trouble, returning two hours later. Shortly afterwards they took off again, this time flying singly down the southern approaches, returning at about 11 am. At 2 pm, nine twin-engine planes took off from Kallang and searched again in the same direction, returning about two hours later.

According to the Naval Board report: 'Apparently they assumed that the attack had been made via the Malacca Straits, and were probably searching for a submarine.'

By 2.30 pm no surface patrol craft were visible in the area. 'It was not until later that they thought of looking over the islands south of Singapore and sent some fighters to make recce.'

The enemy then switched their search to the south and the islands of the Riouw Archipelago and the seaways stretching down to the Sunda Strait between Sumatra and Java, while fighter and other aircraft patrolled Singapore throughout the day.

'A large number of miscellaneous small surface craft worked in the Roads area but the exact nature of the work could not be ascertained. The enemy was certainly caught completely unawares, and almost certainly put the operation down to a submarine.

Having, presumably, failed to locate anything, he may have put a surface patrol onto the Lombok Straits … in an endeavour to close all the passages leading back to Allied bases.'

As the enemy swarmed out of their stronghold in search of the attackers and the search intensified, the four men tried to rest and to overcome the dread that they still had around 70 kilometres to paddle through enemy-infested waters over four nights to reach the *Krait*, if indeed, the *Krait* still even existed. Fortunately the searchers focused on the deep-water approaches to Singapore, based on the likelihood that the attack had been mounted from a submarine. The idea that six enemy canoeists would paddle so far and inflict so much damage evidently did not enter their thinking.

When darkness fell on 27 September the two canoes slipped quietly away from Dongas and headed for the Bulan Strait, Pompong Island and, they hoped, home.

'We expected to encounter difficulties in the form of searchlights and patrols around Sambu, but found that everything was normal,' Lyon wrote. 'Arriving at the north entrance to the Bulan Strait we saw a small steam ship lying at anchor; we drifted past it on the tide without being observed.'

As they were all exhausted they decided to camp at the first suitable place.

'An excellent hide was found, which in daylight proved to be a Chinese graveyard.'

The next night they continued their journey without incident to Bulat and, from there, on to Otter Bay at Pandjang, where they arrived in the middle of a violent storm in the early hours of 30 September.

'We had hoped to cover the first 12 miles [19 kilometres] of the journey to Pompong on the night of the 30th, but heavy cloud banks to the west indicated that there would be another storm, so we decided to postpone our departure till the following morning,' wrote Lyon. 'To risk a day passage of 28 miles [45 kilometres] was a serious decision, but it was amply justified by the violence that later developed.'

They set off the following morning with an interval of one hour between the canoes, paddling all day against a headwind.

'Several aircraft flew over us without displaying any interest and we must have been clearly visible to the OP at Pulau Gual but we arrived without incident at our rendezvous, Pulau Forte, where we rested for an hour before starting out on the remaining 16 miles [26 kilometres] to Pompong.'

Both canoes arrived at Pompong at 3 am on 2 October and circumnavigated the island in search of the *Krait*.

'The agreed rendezvous was between dusk and dawn on October 1/2, but neither canoe could find any trace of her in the anchorage. We therefore slept on the beach until dawn, when we stowed our canoe in the jungle; it was while doing this that we saw *Krait* about two miles [three kilometres] away heading down the Temiang Strait. We then realised that, such had been our fatigue on the previous night, we had paddled to and fro in the anchorage without being able to see the ship.'

One can only imagine how dismayed they must have felt to see the *Krait* sailing away from them. Lyon, in typical fashion, spared no words for such strong emotions in his journal entries. He simply added, 'A search of the island revealed traces of a newly vacated campsite. We therefore considered it likely that Davidson had succeeded in keeping the rendezvous, and knowing the adverse weather conditions of the previous nights would bring back *Krait* at a later date.'

However, the four could not be at all certain that she would return for them, especially since Lyon had originally ordered

Carse to sail on without them if they missed the rendezvous. So they set about planning the next phase of their escape, should she not return.

'Meanwhile, we started to organise ourselves for a stay of several weeks in Pompong,' Lyon wrote. 'Page started to build a hut, and I contacted some friendly Malays, who promised to supply us with fish and vegetables for as long as we should stay on the island. They stated that the Malay inhabitants of the Lingga Archipelago were living in a state of misery, without any supplies of rice, sago or clothing. They further said that they had no interest in who won the war provided that normal trading would be resumed: that under the present conditions the Bugis sailors were afraid to put to sea, resulting in a complete breakdown in trade.

'When asked if it would be possible to smuggle rubber to Australia in return for rice they considered that the Japanese restrictions to navigation east of Ambon were such that this would not be possible.'

* * *

Ted Carse and his seven-man crew aboard the *Krait* had continued to sail in and out of the islands and inlets, doing their best to avoid detection by passing aircraft and maritime vessels and waiting with anxiety for news of the raid to hit the airwaves. By 30 September they still had no idea if their canoeists had managed to blow up any ships or whether they had survived, escaped or been captured. Trepidation was mounting as they began to head towards Pompong Island and the planned rendezvous.

On 1 October, Young reported, 'Today is a memorable day filled with a certain amount of anxiety – we are nearing Singapore and should pick up party about 7 pm. Dawn broke an oily dead

115

calm which boded us evil. Sure enough a storm struck, whipping up heavy seas and as we are running to a split-second timetable it's not too healthy. Sighted a dark object on the surface about five miles [eight kilometres] away, unidentified.

'The time being now 6 pm and we are in the island group of our rendezvous – we are five hours later thanks to the storm and should be in Temiang Strait shortly. We give our Owen guns and pistols the final once-over and check 2 magazines each – all set in case he tries any funny business – it's remarkable the absence of reconnaissance aircraft, last time we were up here there were quite a few. If we survive tonight OK we should be back in Aussie in a fortnight, whacko.'

The *Krait* made it to the rendezvous point five hours late, just after midnight on 2 October.

Carse wrote briefly, 'We made Pompong about 00.20 and dropped a small anchor. Shortly afterwards we saw a canoe approaching. It contained Lieutenant Davidson and Acting AB Falls. They had had a successful trip but had not seen the others since before the event.'

Horrie Young was a little more expansive. Later that day he wrote, 'We arrived at Pompong approximately midnight where Lieut. Davidson and Poppa Falls were awaiting us anxiously. You can imagine the relief on both sides when we met. So far, the other canoes have not turned up and we, after waiting off the island until 6 am, proceeded to sea. The water was extremely deep where we anchored and our main anchor was lost during weighing. The absence of the other two canoes is causing a little worry as they had the least distance to travel. However, Major Lyon was last reported to be weakening rapidly.'

They were all desperate to know whether the other four – Lyon, Huston, Page and Jones – had made it.

The deeply worried Carse added, 'We lay at anchor till daybreak but no sign of the others. As daylight tomorrow (3 October) is the deadline for waiting, if they are not here tonight we won't know what to do. The major [Lyon] said that if still alive by then they would concentrate on taking a sailing vessel and making their way back that way.'

But Carse had no intention of following that particular order of Lyon's. As Young wrote the next day, 'After steaming all night out to sea we have turned about for Pompong in an endeavour to pick them up. If they are not there by tomorrow morning we will steam up to Pandjang, our advance base, and see if they have been there. Failing that we will have to consider them lost and return to Aust, which will be very hard to do under the circumstances. We take a fair amount of risk steaming back all the time as natives may get suspicious – exit *Krait*.'

* * *

Uncertain as to whether they would ever see the *Krait* again, the four remaining canoeists hiding on Pompong Island not only set about making friends with the natives, but also started developing Lyon's backup plan of pirating a native sailing vessel and heading to India on the change of monsoon. Thankfully, they had no need of it.

'Our problems were solved by the return of *Krait* at 2200 hours on 3–4 October,' Lyon wrote with his typical English understatement.

As the *Krait* steamed quietly into the bay in the black night, the men, with great relief, mounted their folboats for the final time and paddled out to salvation.

A jubilant Carse reported: 'Picked up remainder of personnel and returned down Strait. Well we are on our way home. Thank God!'

And Horrie Young wrote: 'Last night a very momentous occasion, the other two canoes had arrived. We picked them up amid much excitement – all exchanging views and adventures.'

He said later, 'I recall Andy Crilly, anticipating their return and the need of solid food, had cooked up a storm of dehydrated mutton stew and navy cocoa which all four new arrivals put away with some gusto before retiring for a long period of well-earned rest.'

After they were dragged aboard the *Krait* by willing hands, for the first time in the history of Operation Jaywick Major Lyon called for drinks all round.

Ted Carse produced a bottle of Beenleigh OP rum – the first booze touched by anyone on board since the *Krait* had left Exmouth – and Bob Page poured it into 14 cups spread out on number 4 hatch. Only Paddy McDowell refused a dram, proclaiming that if he had one he would want 20 and then how would they get home?

When the celebration ended, the six operatives had told their stories and retired for 24 hours of solid sleep. The rest of the crew packed the folboats into their bags and Carse set course for the last time to Temiang Strait and Australia beyond.

'A total of seven ships were sunk aggregating approximately 40,000 tons – in all a very successful expedition,' wrote Horrie Young on 4 October. 'And now for home sweet home – never to see Pompong again, we sincerely hope.'

11

A very close call

As the *Krait* turned for home with all hands present and accounted for, a renewed sense of optimism flowed through the crew.

By 5 October the men were all settling back into shipboard life and their designated roles. Despite the intensive Japanese search for the Singapore saboteurs that included extensive sea and air patrols and interrogations of local inhabitants, it seemed that they might just have pulled it off.

At 6 am Carse wrote in the ship's log: 'Most of the excitement has now died down and we are back to normal routine. The knowledge gained about the defences of Singapore should be invaluable and I will leave that to the reports of Lt Davidson and Maj Lyon. The operation so far has been an unqualified success. All that remains is to return safely with our information.'

Young noted, 'Yesterday afternoon a large four-engine Kawasaki flying boat flew over evidently en-route for Singapore.

He paid us no attention though. I resume [wireless/telegraph] watches and all has settled down to more or less routine – we are headed back to Borneo.'

Like the rest of the crew, Young could not suppress his excitement at the prospect of getting home but he was still very mindful of the potential obstacles that lay ahead. The next day, 6 October, he wrote, 'Pass a large group of islands on our way home just off Borneo coast. We are racing flat out for Lombok Straits and should pass through them on the night of the 10th. It's grand to think that Australia is only nine days ahead of us although we still have the danger of Lombok to contend with. I feel quite confident that we will pass through OK – the only worry is the strong tide flowing [that] the straits have – time will tell.'

The men were blissfully unaware that back in Singapore the brutal Kempei Tai Japanese secret police were rounding up locals as they desperately tried to figure out what had happened in their safe harbour.

* * *

The Japanese high command had no inkling that their citadel had been attacked by a daring band of Allied military operatives from Australia using an old wooden fishing boat, folding canoes and magnetic limpet mines attached with broomsticks.

In the event, locals were blamed and on 10 October 1943 dozens of Singaporeans, including Chinese and westerners, were tortured and at least 15 murdered in what became known as the 'double tenth incident' or 'double tenth massacre' – named for the tenth day of the tenth month. The Kempei Tai's investigation lasted for months as the enemy scrambled to establish who was behind the attack in Keppel Harbour.

One victim of the purge was Elizabeth Choy, who was one of 130 innocent Singaporeans arrested on suspicion and imprisoned and tortured without trial. Her story is told in detail in the biography, *Elizabeth Choy: More than a War Heroine* by Zhou Mei, and it includes horrific details of her treatment at the hands of the Japanese during 193 days in a four-by-three-metre cell that she shared with 20 others. She was slapped, kicked and spat on and even electrocuted. The latter induced a life-long fear of electricity, but despite the torture she refused to confess to something that she had not done.

For her courage she was awarded the Order of the British Empire (OBE) in 1946 – the same year that 21 Japanese military officers were tried for war crimes connected with the incident.

The 'double tenth incident' is commemorated every year in Singapore and on 26 September 2013, the 70th anniversary of Operation Jaywick, the Changi Museum sponsored a special remembrance ceremony attended by several veterans of 'Z' Special Unit.

* * *

Back on board the *Krait*, everyone's thoughts were turning to home and on 11 October Carse wrote: 'We have all painted again except Acting AB Jones who in cases like this acts as a handwaver. He has the build of a Jap and somewhat the same colouring and is to show himself on deck and wave to any inquisitive Japanese plane that might circle around the ship either today, tomorrow or the day after. After that we should be reasonably safe and able to look forward to a good meal and a bottle of beer at Exmouth.'

That day – one week after they had transited the Temiang Strait for the final time and a fortnight after the raid – the

Krait approached the northern entrance to the Lombok Strait, potentially the most hazardous chapter of their homeward journey. Yet despite the close proximity of enemy forces either side on Bali and Lombok and the main Japanese navy and air bases at Surabaya not that far off on the east coast of Java, the officers and crew exuded an almost cocky confidence.

Apart from the treacherous tidal currents the key danger was being intercepted by a Japanese naval patrol vessel, but neither Lyon nor Davidson were concerned about the threat.

They believed, somewhat optimistically given the havoc they had just wreaked in Singapore harbour, that because the strait had not been patrolled on their inbound journey it was unlikely to be patrolled on their way back out, even after the attack.

In his log Carse noted a touch ominously that, 'Today has easily been the clearest day since commencing our return journey and the one day that we really did not need to see at all far. As there is nearly a full moon tonight I hope that it clouds over a little before we enter the strait.'

The crew was now preparing for the worst that, they now knew from experience, the weather and tidal rips of the strait could offer. According to the log: 'We still have about one and a half hours of daylight left before we commence our final running of the gauntlet. As darkness approached we increased speed to our maximum and drove her at it. A fresh south easterly sprang up and the sea was short and very choppy. As we neared the northern narrows we encountered tide rips with the waves breaking all over us. This went on till 2300 when we got into the strait proper and the water was fairly calm.'

This, however, proved to be the proverbial calm before the storm. In his diary, Horrie Young recorded that at 9 pm the boat was going 'hell for leather' with the south-flowing tidal current pushing her through the strait. 'Then, the worst shock of the trip. About midnight each man was silently awakened to the words of "sail bearing down on us". We immediately change course and head for Bali about six miles abeam of us.'

Jones had been on lookout duty on top of the wheelhouse at 11.30 pm when he spotted what he thought was a sail approaching quite fast.

'That's no sail – that ship has a bone between her teeth,' Carse responded in alarm.

The 'sail' was in fact the bow wave of a very large and fast-moving Japanese warship that was rapidly bearing down on them.

The moment they had all dreaded since arriving in enemy waters almost a month earlier had arrived and their thoughts may well have immediately turned to their weapons drills and the cyanide pills.

As the adrenaline surged the crew went to action stations and Horrie Young switched on his radios for what he was sure would be the last time. He waited for Lyon to draft the text of the fateful final signal, along with their estimated position. As he thought about the very possible imminent end of his life, Young also contemplated the large box of plastic explosives that had spent the entire journey on top of his radio set.

'The amount of explosive would have been probably sufficient to have demolished a battleship,' he wrote in his 2004 memoir.

The plan had always been that if the *Krait* was about to be captured by an enemy warship she would manoeuvre in as close as possible to the hostile vessel, then Lyon would detonate the charge, sending the *Krait*, her crew and – they hoped – the enemy ship to 'Davy Jones' locker'.

During an ABC Radio interview with Caroline Jones many years later, she asked Young what would have happened to him if he had hit the detonator button. 'I guess there wouldn't have been a great deal of me left,' was his wry reply.

'It was an experience that I doubt I will ever forget, in fact it still haunts me in my sleep,' he wrote.

Seventy-five years afterwards it remained uppermost in Moss Berryman's mind, too. The sudden possibility of having succeeded in the mission yet being doomed to fail at the last hurdle was lost on nobody.

The fog of war, where memories are blurred by stress and the passage of time, resulted in Young estimating that the enemy vessel stayed alongside the *Krait* for 20 minutes or more, but in the ship's log, Ted Carse recorded that she stayed with them for only about five minutes.

Berryman remembered being woken up and told to break out the Bren gun and keep his head down. He also recalled that the box of plastic explosives, which had been terrorising Horrie Young for weeks, was moved to the bow and the fuse set, with Lyon keeping his finger on the 'button'.

'If this destroyer got too cheeky with hailing us and putting lights on us, we were going to turn, put our nose right against his mid-ships and blow him and us into a million pieces,' Berryman said.

Then, for only the second time during the operation, Lyon broke out the cyanide capsules. Berryman remembered the boss saying, 'Righto boys, if you don't want to be blown up take one of these pills and bite it and that will kill you.'

Carse identified the enemy warship as a destroyer or corvette-type vessel about 70–80 metres long. Amazingly, when she drew alongside the *Krait* she did not challenge the boat or even shine a spotlight on her. For reasons that remain a mystery to this day, to everyone's enormous relief the warship peeled off after several minutes and set a course at high speed towards Lombok Island. Lyon announced with some cautious bravado that the *Krait* had 'won that little war', with her complement of 14 seeing off a ship with probably 200 enemy souls on board.

In his log, Carse noted that it was midnight before the warship was out of sight (and they never took their eyes off her for an instant). 'Whether it was because of the approach to the change of watches and the officer of the first had had a big day and wanted to go to his bunk or they had got into trouble with some high-ranking official over stopping similar boats we can't tell, but it was certainly a miracle. All we could do was to alter course due west and hope for the best and it worked.'

After the run-in with the enemy ship, the tidal rips and heavy seas at the southern end of the Lombok Strait seemed as comfortable as 'sitting before a nice fire', as Carse put it.

At 3.40 am on 12 October the *Krait* motored past the southern tip of Lombok Island and Carse set a course due south in a very rough sea state 6 (waves of 4–6 metres). 'Well if we survive today and tomorrow all should be well, but if possible, we do not want another half hour like last night,' the ship's log comments.

By 7.30 pm and with no sightings of enemy ships or aircraft during the day, Carse was in a more optimistic mood. 'We have just hauled the Japanese ensign down for the last time on this trip. For now, we once again have become an efficient fighting force … It is a grand feeling to be free again on no-man's sea.'

On the evening of 13 October Lyon ordered Horrie Young to break radio silence and send a signal for Admiral Ralph Christie at the Potshot base at Exmouth. Before the mission, Christie had asked Lyon to examine Lombok Strait for evidence of enemy activity and to report his findings as soon as possible. The strait was a popular strategic thoroughfare for American submarines transiting from Australia to the South China Sea.

Lyon passed a coded signal to Young, who tried to raise the naval communications station at HMAS *Coonawarra* in Darwin. The signal provided details of the enemy warship, the success of Operation Jaywick and expected arrival time back at Exmouth. Young said that the call lasted less than one minute but he received no response. So he expressed concern to Lyon about any further attempts given the proximity of enemy air bases on Lombok. 'It was agreed that we should wait 48 hours before making any further calls,' Young recalled in his memoir.

At 6 am on 15 October, under an overcast sky and in an abating sea state, Young made another radio call, which was answered immediately by the AWA commercial coast station operating under naval control in Perth.

'Important day today as I pass the following message to the US Navy station at Fremantle (VIX/0)' noted Young in his diary. '"A.C.N.B. from Krait – mission completed stop for Admiral Christie Lombok now patrolled stop E.T.A. pm seventeenth". It gave me quite a kick talking to folks back in Australia again. All on board were quite excited about it. Another cause for uncertain excitement was the cry, "aircraft", one we all dread. Fortunately it happened to be one of our old "cats" [Catalina flying boats] on a lonely patrol, he never saw us though.'

His message was passed quickly and acknowledged as received by the station.

Young was later criticised in some quarters for breaking radio silence on 13 October, but, as the *Krait*'s log clearly shows, he had simply been acting on orders from Lyon, who was responding to a personal request from Admiral Christie, who wanted to protect his submarine fleet.

Before his death in July 2011, Young was determined to set the record straight about an issue that had worried the professional radio operator for many years. In an interview with Brisbane-based film-maker John Schindler he explained, 'As all naval people know, an enemy report contains certain specific information and must be sent immediately on sighting the enemy, particularly if you're within visual range of the enemy. You don't wait for three or four days before you send an enemy report … I was merely the vehicle to send the message, which was sent in "bull's code", and the code of course was kept by the officer commanding the operation, Ivan Lyon … I was handed the message to transmit and when one is given that instruction, one carries it out, particularly when you're a leading hand.'

'Bull code' was a higher level cryptographic codenamed after the fictional character Ferdinand the bull who in a popular children's story refused to fight. The codename was a reminder to special forces and coast watchers during World War II that their job was to observe rather than to fight.

Young did not know why his initial signal to HMAS *Coonawarra* had not been received, but speculated that it might have been due to a weak signal and lack of a proper antenna after *Krait*'s mast had been stowed, or there might have been strong sunspot activity in the vicinity.

'But as the logbooks show, the instructions were and the directions were logged there that I was to send the signal,' he told Schindler. 'Apparently not everybody has read those instructions.'

On Saturday, 16 October the *Krait* was about 300 kilometres northwest of Exmouth Gulf. At last Young was able to listen to Australian radio stations and to glean some news about how the wider war effort was proceeding.

'We should hit EG [Exmouth Gulf] tomorrow evening and how we are looking forward to it,' his diary reveals. 'Plenty of fresh food, a bed to sleep in, beer etc. and above all tons of fresh water and showers to wash in. It's just going to be like waking up from a nightmare and we can say, "Thank God that's over and done with".'

However, due to a final bout of severe weather, their arrival into Exmouth was delayed and it was not until 2 am on 19 October, 47 days and 7000 kilometres after they had departed, that the *Krait* anchored two miles (three kilometres) east of USS *Chanticleer*.

At 6 am she proceeded alongside *Chanticleer* and according to the ship's log: 'Work immediately commenced on urgent repairs.'

The *Krait* had not only been sent to Singapore to attack enemy shipping. As an essential component of special forces operations behind enemy lines, the raiders were also tasked with gathering intelligence, to be passed back up the line on their return. This they did in meticulous detail, and it proved to be a goldmine of information – not only about the defences in Singapore harbour but much more.

The Naval Board report, classified until 1970, reveals that the Jaywick operatives had taken with them aircraft silhouettes as well as photographs and silhouettes of Japanese merchant ships and more to use as references along with their maps whenever ships or aircraft were seen.

'As a result of this, identification was made immediately the sighting took place, and a log was kept of all sightings and details of identifications, etc. Where sightings could not be identified, sketches were made and these, together with the details, were included in the log.'

The operatives were evidently given little time for celebration when they returned.

'On arrival back at their base [Potshot] the personnel were immediately interrogated and, in spite of the fact that they had identified sightings on the spot, full descriptions of [aircraft], ships etc seen were required to be given, and these details enabled subsequent identification of sightings, and a check was thereby made on both the sightings and Jaywick's interpretation of the characteristics. In all but a few minor cases Jaywick's original identifications were found to be correct.'

In a section of its report titled 'Collated Intelligence', the Naval Board also systematically details all the intelligence on the observed topography including locations, anchorages, tides, rips, waterways, coastlines, beaches, vegetation, water supplies, roads, tracks, proximity of islands; enemy installations, aircraft and shipping movements as well as their types, numbers, dates and times and anything else of military significance; the location and movement of native sailing craft and any 'native' activity.

It was all compiled using both the Jaywick operators' logs and the information provided during their interrogations on returning home. Their intelligence was combed through as they recounted again and again the details of the attacks and what they had observed while they were paddling in and out of the harbour, to squeeze out any further details that they might have forgotten in the heat of the mission. They were also quizzed about their observations of the reactions of the local people to the explosions. It was vital to know whether they were sympathetic to the Japanese occupation – evidently not, at least in some observed cases. Such intelligence would be put to good use in any further covert missions that might be planned in the archipelago.

According to the report: 'The Malays ... on the island of Batam, just behind Dongas, were evidently very jubilant after the attack. They were observed from Dongas, and much laughing and shouting was heard. They appeared to take great delight in imitating the noise of the explosions, while raising both hands upwards and outward presumably in imitation of the effect of the explosions. Other Malays from other areas came out in their boats to view the fires and the pall of smoke hanging over the target areas. It must [have] recalled to their memories a similar sight of Singapore at the time of capitulation. Canoe 2 [Davidson and Falls], having landed on the [northeast] coast of Batam Island (27 Sep) on the return journey in order to shelter from a storm, were approached by two Malays in a kelek [raft], evidently with the same intention in mind. The latter, however, when they got near to the beach evidently caught sight of the two white men (the canoe was well hidden) and turned tail and fled. They may have associated the sight with the explosions and thought it wiser not to get mixed up in such things.'

Apart from that and Lyon's meeting with the old Malay on Pompong, 'no contact was made with the local peoples' the report says.

The 14 men of Operation Jaywick and their chief organiser, Major Jock Campbell, would be reunited one more time in early December 1943 at the 'Z' staging camp in Jordan Terrace, Brisbane. A nine–gallon (34-litre) keg of beer was consumed over lunch before the men scattered to their various units.

Despite the fact that one of the key objectives of the mission had been to generate propaganda value and to show the public and the allies that the Japanese were not invincible, the raid was kept quiet. The secrecy caused a lot of pain for people in Singapore but was deemed necessary given plans for future similar clandestine raids.

12

The Rimau six

During their time in Brisbane celebrating the success of Operation Jaywick, Ivan Lyon approached each man to ask if he would be interested in having another crack at the enemy in Singapore with a second raid.

Five of the Jaywick operatives – Davidson, Page, Falls, Marsh and Huston – agreed to join Lyon and were on the team for Operation Rimau, the second planned surprise attack against Singapore a year later. Of the six, only Marsh had not been chosen to paddle into the harbour during Jaywick. He had been bitterly disappointed to be left behind on the *Krait* as a reserve canoeist. Of the six original canoeists on Jaywick, only Jones declined Lyon's offer to return as part of Operation Rimau.

Rimau is the Malay word for 'tiger' and Lyon carried a large tiger's head tattoo on his chest. The mission was sanctioned by his masters at the SOE in London and supported by Australian and American commanders.

Tragically, the six Jaywick men and another 17 Allied operatives on the mission would all be killed in action, die in captivity or be brutally executed in Singapore by the Japanese after a sham trial.

The operation had been compromised on 6 October 1944. Ivan Lyon and Donald Davidson died in action while Andrew 'Happy' Huston drowned during their fighting withdrawal. Lyon and Davidson were killed together on 14 October in a skirmish with a superior Japanese force on Soreh Island, to the east of the route they had taken during Jaywick. Fred 'Boof' Marsh died from wounds and illness soon after he arrived back in Singapore in December 1944.

Their fates had been sealed when the British submarine HMS *Tantalus*, under the command of Lieutenant Commander Hugh Mackenzie, deliberately failed to turn up on the agreed date to rescue the men. There is also a large question mark over whether or not United States intelligence intercepts, that might have saved the men, were withheld from British and Australian authorities.

Regardless of what might have been, on 7 July 1945 – just a month before the end of the Pacific War – Bob Page and Walter 'Poppa' Falls, with eight other Rimau operatives, were beheaded in cold blood in Singapore, close to the site of a modern-day golf course, by troops from the 7th Area Army Headquarters.

Lyon's two closest confidants, Donald Davidson and Bob Page, had both had serious reservations about the complexity of the plan for Operation Rimau, which involved a submarine transit from Australia, the capture of a local junk and an insertion into Singapore harbour using largely untested one-man submersible craft called Sleeping Beauties. Neither man was overly keen to participate in the operation, but neither would allow Lyon to go without them.

Twenty-five-year-old Captain Page, who had married his sweetheart, Roma Prowse, at St Andrew's Church in Canberra following Operation Jaywick, told a friend, 'Ivan's crazy, but I can't let him go on his own; I can't let him down. But this raid will be my last.' How right he was.

The executions of Page and Falls were confirmed by military authorities on 18 October 1945.

'These men were imprisoned in Outram Road gaol Singapore at the end of June or beginning of July this year,' the official report held by the National Archives says. 'On the orders of the Japanese general staff they were removed from the gaol on 7 July, 1945 and taken out to the waste area near the reformatory school where they were beheaded. Their remains are buried in three graves to the east of the road. Each grave is marked with two wooden crosses.'

Horrie Young went to his grave in 2011, convinced that he had been saved from certain death on Operation Rimau by an administrative hiccup: the 50 per cent salary loading that he was supposed to receive upon joining the SRD had never been paid to him.

'While I thought it was rather a shabby trick at the time, I have ever since had cause to thank those responsible for welching on the deal because I believe they unwittingly saved my life. I feel reasonably sure that had the allowance been restored I would have remained with that organisation and most probably joined the Rimau party,' he wrote in his 2004 memoir.

Instead, Young was transferred to the new SRD training camp at Fraser Island before returning to navy duty in 1944. He was demobbed in mid-1946 and like Carse, Berryman, Marsh and Cain he was awarded a Mentioned in Dispatches (MID) for the performance of their duties. The citation says their 'great cheerfulness and bearing throughout was of the highest standard in most trying and hazardous conditions'.

For their courage and devotion to duty the other Jaywick men were awarded the following: Lyon, Davidson and Page the Distinguished Service Order (DSO); McDowell, Falls, Jones and Huston the Distinguished Service Medal (DSM); and Morris and Crilly the Military Medal (MM).

The citation for Andy Crilly's medal states that his 'general bearing, cheerfulness and devotion to duty in most difficult and dangerous conditions were of the highest standard throughout'. Crilly received his 'gong' in 1946 after he had returned to his home in the Lockyer Valley near Ipswich in Queensland to work on local farms. He ran unsuccessfully as a Labor candidate in the State election and died in September 1963. He is buried at Ipswich cemetery.

Following Operation Rimau, Lieutenant Colonel Lyon was recommended posthumously for the Victoria Cross (VC) for his 'gallantry and determination' by none other than the Australian Prime Minister, John Curtin, on advice from the commander-in-chief of Australian forces, General Sir Thomas Blamey. Unfortunately, the British authorities only upgraded his Jaywick DSO to a Distinguished Service Cross (DSC), the second-highest Imperial award for valour by an officer after the VC.

His citation for the Jaywick DSC says that 'Lyon's coolness and resourcefulness in the face of the enemy, and the example of confidence and disregard for personal safety set by him in his leadership of the party were the main factors in the complete success of the expedition.'

Bob Page was originally recommended for a Military Cross but his award was upgraded to a DSO.

Horrie Young's son, Brian, who had been born on the very day that Operation Jaywick began, said that his father always believed that Ted Carse should have been given a higher honour. Born in Petersham in Sydney, Brian spent many hours with his father in his later years as he recounted the voyage to Singapore and back on what the navy veteran regarded as the happiest ship he ever served on.

Speaking on the deck of a holiday villa overlooking the sparkling junction of the Bellinger and Kalang rivers at Urunga (his mum's hometown) on the New South Wales mid-north coast in late 2017, Brian Young recalled with great pride that his father had remained good friends with Carse long after the war was over.

Brian Young said his father had the highest regard for the tough old salt whom he regarded as one of the finest seamen he had ever met. He also thought highly of Ivan Lyon and supported the idea of both men being awarded the VC.

'Dad said he [Ted] was the only officer on board after the canoeists had left; he had to take the vessel around, keep it out of sight, patrol around, make it look like it was a local vessel and he had a very young crew,' he said. 'The only one who had any age on him was Paddy McDowell and he was the stoker – and the rest of them he said were mainly 18-, 19-, 20-year olds playing jokes and having fun. Ted had to put up with all that sort of thing and Dad said he rarely ever raised his voice. He said he was more like a father figure, I suppose.'

Brian Young added that his dad was disgusted at one suggestion that Donald Davidson held a revolver to Ted Carse's belly to make him return for the late raiders.

'Dad said that was absolute hogwash and apart from anything else it was not in Davidson's nature to do something like that,' he said. 'In fact, Davidson slept for 20 hours after he returned to the *Krait* and during that time Ted had made the vessel ready to return for the other four.'

Horrie Young said there was no doubt that Carse had disobeyed Lyon's order not to wait for stragglers, but no one, least of all the survivors, ever pulled him up on it.

Another criticism of Carse was that he suffered from nervous tension, but Horrie Young dismissed that out of hand. His evidence was the time when Carse coolly stopped in broad daylight and within sight of other vessels and ordered the crew over the side to scrape the *Krait*'s hull, which was covered in weed that was slowing her down.

'To me, that doesn't sound like a man that was nervous,' Horrie pointed out.

During the post-Jaywick festivities in Brisbane, when Ivan Lyon interviewed each member of the crew individually and asked them if they wanted to join him for another mission to Singapore, he emphasised that he would not hold it against them if they said no.

Moss Berryman remembered thinking for 'about two seconds' before declining Lyon's kind offer. 'Luckily, I was one of those who said "No".'

Berryman spent the remainder of the war in general navy service with most of his time on board the destroyer HMAS *Vendetta* patrolling off New Guinea.

'When the war ended, I came back to South Australia to get out of the navy and just to finish up. One morning – it was the day before Christmas – we were told to pack our bags. "You're on the Melbourne express, you're going to Melbourne tonight, Christmas Eve." We looked at one another – there was about 40 of us. We said, "We're not going back to Flinders Naval Depot, this is Christmas Eve, we're not going anywhere, we've just been examined, our teeth are still there and we've still got all our body parts, you can't do much about it, we're not going, it's Christmas Eve." And we didn't go on Christmas Eve but we did go the next morning back to *Cerberus* [the RAN base on the Mornington Peninsula].

'When we got over there, we said to a mob of lads who had just come in from somewhere, "What goes on around here?" and they said, "Well, we're going home but you're taking over from us". We said, "Well, what are you doing?" "Oh, we're driving trucks, we've all got a rake and a shovel, we're making a golf course for the officers." So we spent another week back in *Cerberus* driving trucks and making a golf course and then finally, at the end of December we were back in Adelaide and that was the end of the story as far as the navy goes.'

After the war Moss Berryman returned to his old job with the stockbroking firm SC Ward & Co, where he spent the next 46 years until his retirement. He married his nursing sister sweetheart, Mary, and they had four daughters.

In 1993, on the fiftieth anniversary of Operation Jaywick, then 70-year-old Berryman was at Kranji War Cemetery in Singapore paying his respects to his fallen comrades. Seventeen of the 23 Operation Rimau operatives are buried in that cemetery. He was standing over the grave of Lieutenant Colonel Ivan Lyon, DSC when Lyon's son, Clive, who had never known his father, moved in beside him. 'He was a dead ringer for his father with short curly hair and a pipe in his mouth. He said to me, "What was my father like?"' Berryman recalled.

'I said, "Why do you ask?"'

'He said, "I've been told he was really hard, you couldn't get on with him and he couldn't get on with some of the boys, they just wouldn't play ball." I said, "Well you can forget all that rubbish;

if he said you were going to go for a paddle for five miles [eight kilometres], ten miles [16 kilometres], 20 miles [32 kilometres], he was with you all the way. Not once did we ever query anything he said; not once did we get the feeling that we'd like to pull out and go back into general service". He said, "Good, I'm pleased that you've said that." We both had tears because he didn't know his father, being just a baby at the time.'

AFTER JAYWICK

13

Small force, big impact

The essence of special forces operations is to apply the lowest number of troops to a task to achieve the maximum impact.

Audacity is the crucial element of the 'Who Dares Wins' motto of the SAS, while 'Strike Swiftly' and 'Without Warning' are the mantras of the army's two Commando regiments. All these terms apply equally to Operation Jaywick and the men of 'Z' Special Unit: it was certainly a daring mission, which they won after striking swiftly and without warning.

The ties between early special operations units such as 'Z' Special Unit and modern-day special forces are more than just historic; they are ingrained in the very nature of the unconventional work these fighters are trained to do. The operators of today, who survive the tests of extreme hardship and endurance that are required simply to be selected for special forces duty, share a powerful bond with the members of SOA during World War II.

Speaking in his large, sparsely furnished office overlooking Lake Burley Griffin in Canberra in October 2017, with Parliament House framed by the distant blue of the Brindabella Range, the then chief of the Australian Army, Lieutenant General Angus Campbell, said Operation Jaywick is a classic example of what can be achieved by a small, well-trained force.

'Their impact, I think most particularly, was psychological,' he said. 'And that can on occasions be as dramatic as physical effect.'

As a former SAS officer as well as a senior civilian public servant, General Campbell, who became Chief of the Defence Force in July 2018, understands the intricate machinery of Australian government and politics better than most military officers. His name became more widely known to the public during his term as the commander of Operation Sovereign Borders. This was when the government and its then Immigration Minister Scott 'stop the boats' Morrison controversially shut down all information on asylum seekers by applying an unprecedented level of censorship – an official silence under the banner of 'on-water matters'.

Angus Campbell grew up in an army family and attended numerous schools as his soldier father moved around the country. He spent his final two high school years at St Gregory's Marist Brothers College at Campbelltown on the outskirts of Sydney.

After he moved from the 'big' army to the special forces world, Campbell was introduced to the story of Operation Jaywick and the exploits of 'Z' Special Unit as well as the other top-secret units from World War II.

'I became familiar with them once I had entered into SAS and you were encouraged to get to know the history, the folklore and the influence of special forces throughout Australia's history – to see that it's not just in the European theatre of the Second World War, but also in the Pacific theatre. That's where Operation Jaywick, and the service of those who sailed the *Krait*, became well known and a great point of encouragement and sense of recognition of what you can do, if you put your mind to it, in terms of small forces making a significant impact.'

Campbell calls the Jaywick mission a textbook example of the boldness of special operations to go where the enemy finds it inconceivable that such a mission would even be attempted. 'It showed that our special forces' potential and reality was just as impressive as those emerging in the European theatre.'

He stresses that most special forces operations are inherently difficult and often almost impossible to pull off: 'The planning is incredibly important and a large component of luck and opportunity and an ability to seize a moment, they all lead to the perceptions of public success or not,' he said. 'I think regardless of a particular mission, it is that audacity; that willingness to dare that's the spirit of seeking to take the fight to your enemy and to unbalance the enemy; make them question where are they going to be attacked next and to what degree they can singularly focus on their plans or have to be countering and preparing for ours.

'For example, although the second mission organised by Ivan Lyon, Operation Rimau, was a disaster for all concerned, it still had a potent psychological effect. But that mission was doomed from the start, using untried technology and a risky plan in a region whose security had been boosted by many more enemy eyes and ears in the wake of Operation Jaywick.

'If you don't plan it, if you don't train and prepare for it and rehearse it and then conduct it with a degree of bravado and all-in commitment, then you're not going to give your best,' Campbell said. 'You need to anticipate being surprised and be prepared to respond. I would acknowledge, and I think it's really important too, that these then-young men who conducted these operations in the Second World War were tough, resilient, determined and they knew exactly what would happen to them if things didn't go successfully. They were very, very brave.'

According to the 1998 newsletter of the New South Wales 'Z' Special Unit Association, more than 380 'Z' operatives were inserted behind enemy lines during the war and about a quarter were killed. It was courage combined with the determined and somewhat unusual leadership skills of Ivan Lyon that resulted in the success of Jaywick and the audacity of the ultimately doomed Rimau.

'People of strong and in some cases idiosyncratic leadership skills and ideas, there's a moment of opportunity for them. And there's no doubt not only was there a leader [in Lyon] but there was a man who had imagination and who was driven to deliver,' Campbell said.

He said that a crucial element of leadership is the team ethos established by the commander and his ability to select the right type of individuals for a mission. 'I think that building the team is about not only learning what the members of the team can do and how they can be relied upon and each relying on the other, but also the team learning to understand and build a sense of faith and commitment to the leader.

'Then there is that moment when the orders are revealed – and all of the training and the mission purpose and sense of national threat telescopes into a moment of decision for everybody that, yes, this is a team; we are committed to our mission and we're going to do it. And to their great credit, that's exactly the men they were.'

Former SAS major Jim Truscott is a classic and slightly offbeat special forces officer in the mould of World War II renegade

British commander Major General Orde Wingate, who operated behind the lines in Burma with his native Chindit forces.

Thinking well outside the square is a feature common to both men and the ever-thoughtful Truscott also regards Rimau as a successful psychological operation, because it showed the enemy that they were vulnerable.

Truscott spent many months operating alongside rebel forces in the mountains of East Timor in the late 1990s and while he does not downplay the significance of the physical blow to enemy shipping inflicted by the Jaywick canoeists, he too put greater emphasis on the importance of the psychological blow.

There had been a precedent in terms of some of the tactics they used. The British had conducted a similar mission using a mother ship and canoes in West Africa several years before Jaywick, when commandos had 'stolen' a German ship from a neutral port in what was regarded by many as an act of piracy.

While modern–day special forces are bound to act within the rules of war and their legally binding rules of engagement, such niceties did not apply to Wingate or Ivan Lyon during a period of total war.

'It was the attack on the Japanese psyche which was where the blow was delivered,' Truscott said. 'The most successful thing out of Jaywick, to put it into perspective, was not the sinking of the ships, it was the dispersion of the fleet which was the strategic outcome. It caused the Japs humongous angst. When the pinprick happened again [Rimau] they realised they were vulnerable, so the kinetic [physical] stuff [is] irrelevant compared to the psychological blow in both operations. Blow and counterblow is the way I describe it psychologically.'

Truscott said Jaywick also gave the Australian and Allied high command tremendous confidence. 'It's called "Psychological

Consolidation Ops". It's when you build up your own confidence. The fact that Blamey would have known, MacArthur would have known, not many people in the High Command would have known but it would have said, "We've done something, we've struck the Japanese",' he said.

Rick Moor spent 24 years of his 40-year army career in the special forces world. Born and bred at Warialda in northern New South Wales, he graduated as a young infantry officer in 1976 and served for two years with the Second/Fourth battalion in Townsville before successfully undertaking SAS selection and spending two years attached to US special forces. His final deployment was to the coalition forces Special Operations headquarters in Kabul, Afghanistan, as a full colonel. These days he runs the ACT branch of the SAS Association.

It was in the early 1980s when Moor first met veterans of the Second/Second Independent Company and 'Z' Special Unit, as well as the New Zealand–born SOE operative and war hero Nancy Wake, the famous 'White Mouse' who spent years spying on and killing Germans behind enemy lines in France during World War II. She was on the Gestapo's most-wanted list and at one point in 1944 after she parachuted back into France she had a 5-million-franc bounty on her head.

The diminutive Wake would often visit SAS headquarters in Perth or the top-secret Swan Island spy training facility in Port Phillip Bay near Geelong, where she would regale trainers and trainees alike with tales of her wartime heroics over a bottle or two of gin and single malt.

'I did know Nancy and had several long discussions with her,' Moor said. Importantly, he also got to know Jaywick veterans Taffy Morris and Moss Berryman.

Speaking over coffee in the AWM's café, he said that he regards both Jaywick and Rimau as paramount examples of the 'mythology' of special forces operations.

'A lot of military operations, in terms of the morale of your force, are based to some degree on mythology,' Moor said. 'So, from a mythology point of view, they are the paramount special operations – both Jaywick and then subsequently Rimau – simply because of the daring, tenacity, endurance and courage shown by the men involved.

'It was beyond exceptional and that includes Rimau. Even though the raid was compromised and from that perspective was a failure, the courage shown in the fighting withdrawal over thousands of kilometres is quite remarkable and in the annals of military history it is right up there. So, from that perspective they are the foundation stone of Australian special operations today in terms of "This is what can be done and this is what is possible".'

Most of the more than 280 missions conducted by 'Z' Special Unit and other top-secret units under the umbrella of the SRD and SOA during World War II were so highly classified that they remained unknown to the broader community for decades. Many were also abject failures and some details remain scant even to this day.

Like Truscott, Moor believes that special operations missions are driven personally and that Ivan Lyon drove both Jaywick and Rimau using his force of personality and well-placed connections. As both an army officer and an operative with Britain's overseas spy agency, MI6, Lyon also had deep ties with the top-secret British SOE prior to the fall of Singapore.

'He was really serving with MI6 prior to the outbreak of war and there were other elements of MI6 that were involved in the pre-operations who were in Singapore, and they were also preparing for "stay behind" operations,' Moor said. 'I think the raids were more driven by Ivan Lyon than by a broader British scheme and in typical British fashion, it's often who you know rather than what you know that's important.'

Fortunately, the Australian commander General Sir Thomas Blamey was also a strong supporter of unconventional warfare. 'Blamey was happy to have anyone who was willing to hit back, have a go. It was a small risk in terms of the number of people involved in the bigger picture, and it showed a political alignment with the British.'

Moor said the greatest challenge facing military planners and operators in Australia is always the 'tyranny of distance'.

'When you talk about operational and strategic distances in Australia, it's thousands and thousands of kilometres and to do that, you need a force projection capability and that's what we've always lacked. From a special operations point of view, we have never had that as an organic capability except in 1945.'

Peter Collins is a former Army Reserve commando, ex-naval officer and one-time leader of the New South Wales Liberal Party. He is also on the Council of the ANMM and supports the *Krait*'s long-term preservation at the museum.

Collins is a military history buff and has even built his own small military museum at his historic property near Penrith in far-western Sydney. Taking pride of place in the display is the suspended frame of a folboat canoe, similar to the ones used on the mission.

He believes that the story of the *Krait* and Operation Jaywick has been vastly underplayed in both the formal military education sense and in the wider public understanding of Australia's military history.

'If the *Krait* had been an American ship, it would have been immortalised; it would have been taught in schools, it would have been a fundamental part of the American story,' Collins said. 'Even the British, with the movie *The Cockleshell Heroes* which commemorated the raid by eight or ten Royal Marine commandos on German shipping in Bordeaux, that was nothing compared to the achievement of *Krait*.

'I mean, the south coast of Britain to Bordeaux would have been barely a training exercise for *Krait*. It was almost a local operation in Europe by our standards, Portsmouth to Bordeaux. The equivalent distance for *Krait* was London to Athens – and so in European terms, [from] one end of Europe to the other. That's what our Operation Jaywick achieved with zero casualties and a very comparable amount of shipping destroyed and every bit as much psychological impact.

'For the Bordeaux raid, they were delivered by submarine across Pittwater by our standards. On the *Krait* they were just on display on the ocean on the open seas for weeks on end. There was no backup plan, there were no spares, there was no triple redundancy on *Krait*. If something broke they had to be able to fix it.'

Collins is mystified about why the Jaywick story is so little known across the broader Australian community. 'If you're interested in special forces and Australian military history, you will know about Operation Jaywick and the *Krait* ... but I think a much broader audience needs to understand the national significance of *Krait* and where it positions Australia in the region,' Collins said. 'This talks to not just our past, but our future. This is where we sit in Asia and where the ADF [Australian Defence Force] needs to be capable of operating.

'I'm not suggesting there'll be raids on Singapore harbour again, but it will be over those sorts of distances, and that's what we need to get our heads around. We need to understand: this is where we live, not Europe – and we need to understand our backyard more intimately and we need to know what we've done.

'These days you would insert such a force by submarine or you would drop inflatables out of the back of a C17, you know, 50 miles [80 kilometres] off, and go in from there. Talk about doing it the hard way! Jaywick could not have been harder – and the longer they took to get there, the more exposed they were and the more dangerous it was.'

Collins thinks the *Krait* is by far and away the most important floating exhibit in the ANMM's collection.

'The most significant boat is that little matchstick boat, but it needs to be pulled out of the water, put up in lights and it needs to be interpreted in its wartime guise,' he said. 'I think it's the museum's intention to get it out of the water and to re-equip it for Jaywick. People may not be able to walk on board the ship, but if they can walk on gantries and gangways above the ship and see the equipment, see the commando canoes, see some of the limpet mines, see the weapons they carried, the sorts of uniforms they had, I think that will start to bring it alive. It really needs to be re-equipped to help tell that story.

'*Krait* is as significant to Australian special forces – and this is really the future of the Australian Defence Force – as [HMS] *Victory* was to the Royal Navy. And just as *Victory* has been constantly refitted and rebuilt, I think *Krait* needs to be treated equally respectfully.'

14

What the *Krait* did next

After Operation Jaywick the *Krait* was officially transferred to the Darwin-based maritime arm of SOA.

Or, as Horrie Young put it, 'In case you may think that that was the end of the Jaywick clan's adventures, such was not the case. Lieut. Davidson came back after a couple of weeks and informed us that we would be required to sail *Krait* up to Darwin and hand her over to another clandestine organisation.'

This carried the unlikely codename of the 'Lugger Maintenance Section' but was a veritable flotilla of civilian craft and other specialised military vessels that were used for clandestine wartime operations that were being mounted in the northern chain.

A reduced crew of 11 men sailed the *Krait* to Darwin from Exmouth in late 1943 and handed her over to the section's commanding officer, Captain Jack Chipper.

The other three Jaywick operatives were busy elsewhere. Major Lyon was debriefing with the top brass in Melbourne, Lieutenant Page was marrying his sweetheart, Roma Prowse, in Canberra and Taffy Morris was receiving medical attention in Perth for the shrapnel wound he sustained when the tomato sauce bottle was blasted by the accidental shot during the mission.

Before handing her over, Davidson instructed the crew to remove everything they could from the *Krait*, except for her chronometer and compass, according to Horrie Young.

'I cast around for something to remind me of Jaywick. It was at this point that I happened to notice a small vice fitted to the aft engine room hatchway. I chose to remove it as it was no longer required for use by our party and it seemed to be a useful and worthwhile reminder of Operation Jaywick.'

That vice is still owned by Horrie's son, Brian.

The Lugger Maintenance Section was operated by the SRD and included an array of vessels ranging from folding canoes to high-speed British-designed and Australian-built attack boats known as Fairmiles. These craft, built at the famous Lars Halvorsen yard at Ryde on the Parramatta River in New South Wales and at several other boatyards, were capable of upwards of more than 20 knots and were used to land 'special' operatives throughout the Southwest Pacific Area of Operations.

Other vessels in the section's fleet of more than 20 boats included Harbour Defence Motor Launches (HDMLs) and four 20-metre-long 'snake class' modified and heavily armed wooden fishing boats. They resembled Malay or Chinese fishing vessels and were used to land operatives on beaches and up estuaries throughout New Guinea, Timor, Sulawesi and Borneo. At sea, they were supported by three large 40-metre-long mother ships.

SRD also operated a small air force with RAAF Catalina

flying boats, Liberator bombers and single-engine Auster aircraft seconded for many operations. The Auster 16 Air Observation Flight was under the command of Flight Lieutenant Fred Chaney (later Sir Frederick) who was awarded the Air Force Cross (AFC) for his 'courage, skill and resourcefulness' during the daring rescue mission of American airmen in North Borneo.

Flight Lieutenant Chaney's citation says that he flew his Auster aircraft into the jungle and landed on a 75-yard (69-metre) airstrip that had been built by the local Dyak people. The plane crashed on take-off and Chaney, assisted by the natives, managed to repair it with 'cane and bamboo' and flew out.

'He succeeded in flying four personnel to Tarakan over 300 miles [483 kilometres] of enemy held territory and continued operations from Labuan when it was captured ultimately evacuating the remaining members of the crew,' it reads. 'Flight Lieutenant Chaney has shown exceptional skill and courage in flying unarmed light aircraft over enemy territory.'

While the *Krait* is the best known of the section's vessels, others, such as the minor motorboat the *Kuru*, conducted some extraordinary top-secret operations.

According to records held by the Australian War Memorial, in early 1942 the *Kuru*, with the patrol vessel *Vigilant*, operated the 'Timor Ferry Service' carrying commandos from Sparrow Force, refugees, arms and supplies on 6000-kilometre round trips between Fremantle in Western Australia and isolated bays along the coast of Timor.

The slow-moving *Krait* was an excellent addition to the rag-tag fleet.

The boat's benign fishing-boat design allowed what was now the newly commissioned navy vessel HMAS *Krait* to conduct a variety of SRD missions in the islands to Australia's north between

1943 and the end of the war. These included ferrying personnel and supplies to Timor, Ambon and Morotai.

During this period, she also underwent a minor refit and was captained by Sub Lieutenant Harry Williams, who took her on her first agent pick-up mission to Timor. Fittingly, in August 1945 she was ordered to the island of Ambon in company with HMAS *Bundaberg* to attend the formal surrender ceremony by Japanese forces to the Australian commander, General Sir Thomas Blamey.

The *Krait*'s name was also given to a small bay on tiny Browse Island 180 kilometres northwest of the Kimberley coast, which was a staging post for SRD agents operating between Darwin and Timor.

With the end of hostilities on 2 September 1945 came the inevitable question of what to do with the Lugger Maintenance Section's odd fleet of vessels as they were no longer required as military vessels.

The *Krait* was decommissioned soon afterwards at the island of Labuan off the northwest coast of Borneo. She might have simply disappeared into the annals of history but for a remarkable chain of events that led to her rediscovery.

Rumour had it that she was sold to an unknown buyer who used her to run drugs and weapons around the South China Sea region. She eventually arrived back in Singapore and was left to rot until a Borneo-based sawmiller, Richard Barrett, purchased the boat for his company, The River Estates, and sailed her to Sandakan harbour on the north coast of Borneo.

Barrett, who had been interned by the Japanese at Kota Kinabalu and later at Kuching in Sarawak, renamed the boat the ML *Pedang* (Malay for 'Sword'). For the next decade she was employed by his timber and cocoa operation, hauling logs and moving personnel and supplies to and from Barrett's camps up and down the Kinabatangan, Segama and Dagat rivers to the south of Sandakan.

Barrett's sons, Richard and James, both live in Western Australia. Speaking in early 2018, they recalled spending their school holidays from Aquinas College, Perth, travelling into the timber camps on board the *Pedang* or one of their father's other boats that were also named after traditional weapons – *Beujak* (Spear), *Criss* (Dagger) and *Sumpitan* (Blowpipe).

James Barrett, who followed his father into the timber business after completing a mechanical engineering degree at the University of Western Australia, has vivid memories of the rough ocean crossing from Sandakan to the calm rivers during the monsoon season. The family had moved to Sandakan in 1956 when James was just seven years old.

'I remember it was quite a slim wooden boat and it required a lot of maintenance because it was quite old,' he said. 'My father docked it twice a year for servicing, including caulking the timbers.'

Apart from examining her engines, James Barrett only travelled on the *Pedang* twice.

'It was getting to the end of its life when he would just have burned it. We scuttled the others but managed to sell the *Pedang*,' he recalled. The last time James saw the vessel was in January 1964, just before she was transshipped to Brisbane as deck cargo.

His brother, Richard, was just 13 when he first joined the vessel during his school holidays, but he has mixed memories about the log-shifting business.

'My dad used the boat to pull about 115 teak logs at a time down the river and to the sea and on to the mill,' he said. 'It took about 24 hours but I only went on the trip twice and I didn't like it much because of the seasickness.'

Richard knew very little of the *Krait*'s colourful history until he saw the telemovie *The Heroes* and he thought nothing more about her until a few years ago when he was walking through Darling Harbour in Sydney with his wife.

'I saw the boat moored at the museum and I couldn't believe it. I spoke with the man working on board and told him the story, that I had last seen it in 1962 when I was 13.'

Like his brother, Richard recalled that their father wanted to burn the *Pedang* (*Krait*) because she was becoming difficult and costly to maintain. Fortunately, fate stepped in.

In late 1962 two Sydney timber buyers, Steve Stevenson of Tenaru Timbers, and Max Hayman from Hayman & Ellis, were on a buying trip to British North Borneo when they noticed a vessel in Sandakan harbour that looked remarkably like the *Krait* but carried the name ML *Pedang*.

Both Stevenson and Hayman had been attached to SRD during the war and Stevenson had also been the president of the 'Z' Special Unit Association. They approached Richard Barrett (senior) through a local British police inspector, John Walne, who had also been with SRD. They were then able to confirm that the ML *Pedang* was indeed the former *Kohfuku Maru*, *Suey Sin Fah*, MV *Krait* and HMAS *Krait* – and possibly the most famous Australian vessel of World War II. Barrett told the men that he had changed the name due to her rather unsavoury postwar reputation as a drug runner before he had put her to honest work in his timber business.

Tremendously excited, Stevenson and Hayman returned to Sydney and notified the 'Z' Special Unit Association of their amazing discovery. And so, on their next trip to North Borneo, the pair carried the authority to negotiate with Barrett for the purchase of the ML *Pedang*.

After some persuasion over lunch with the Governor of British North Borneo and Inspector Walne, Barrett agreed to sell the vessel to the association for 30,000 Malay dollars (about £4000 in 1963) and payment was made on 27 December 1963.

The deed of sale, dated March 1964, names The River Estate as vendor and 'Z' Special Unit Association Trustees Major General Sir Denzil Macarthur-Onslow, Rupert Guy Herps (the brother of Douglas and also a 'Z' Special Unit veteran), and Raymond Charles Irish as the buyers.

The P&O line, which had transhipped the *Krait* to Sydney from India in 1943, again came to the party and shipped her from Borneo to Brisbane free of charge as deck cargo on board the freighter *Nellor*.

15

Back to Refuge Bay

The *Krait* was refurbished in Brisbane, where Andy Crilly's widow, Patricia, and their five children paid her a visit before she set sail for Refuge Bay on the Hawkesbury River, on the first leg of her journey to Sydney Harbour, under the command of Harold Nobbs from the Royal Volunteer Coastal Patrol (RVCP). Also on board were the Jaywick skipper Lieutenant Ted Carse along with crew members Horrie Young and Joe Jones. Before she left Broken Bay on Anzac Day, 25 April 1964, the ashes of former Jaywick engineer Paddy McDowell were scattered at sea.

Harold Nobbs had served with naval intelligence during the war as a lieutenant with the Royal Australian Navy Volunteer Reserves (RANVR). Before the war he was a friend of Commander Cocky Long, who would become head of Naval Intelligence and a liaison officer for Britain's MI5 and MI6 intelligence agencies. Long believed that Sydney was vulnerable to attack and had asked Lieutenant Nobbs to form the RVCP and to muster civilian vessels into a kind of 'Dad's Navy' to patrol the harbour.

Also on the *Krait* that day, for the final leg into Sydney Harbour, was yachting journalist Lou d'Alpuget from *The Sun* newspaper (the father of writer Blanche d'Alpuget who would later marry former Prime Minister Bob Hawke). Lou d'Alpuget had been a prime mover for a huge 'save the *Krait*' fundraising program. Money had poured in from grateful people all over Australia, every one of them keen to bring her home.

At Sydney Heads, they were joined by a fourth surviving Jaywick operative, Moss Berryman, for the journey up the harbour. A flotilla of hundreds of spectator craft escorted the battered old ship to her berth, a pontoon moored near the Man O'War Steps in Farm Cove.

The *Krait* arrived to much pomp and fanfare at the pontoon at 3.30 pm. She was met by Sydney Lord Mayor Harry Jensen and the Governor of New South Wales Lieutenant General Sir Eric Woodward. Declaring the vessel a floating war memorial, the Governor officially handed her over to the RVCP, to be used primarily as a training vessel.

* * *

During the next 20 years the *Krait* became a familiar sight on Pittwater north of Sydney. To begin with, many of the older locals in the tight-knit Pittwater community knew her amazing story but as time went on she was taken more for granted, as just a strange-looking vessel moored at the patrol's Church Point headquarters. She was also used as a prop for TV shows and movies such as the ABC's *Patrol Boat* and the Peter Weir film, *Gallipoli*.

During the 1970s the boat was used variously by sea cadets and boy scouts, as a rescue vessel. Her former skipper, ex-navy man and Coastal Patrol volunteer Bill Cockbill, recalled that she also hosted safe-boating courses sponsored by *The Sun* newspaper, with some 1500 people a year undertaking courses in seamanship, boat-handling and navigation.

The *Krait* made visits to other ports for special events, including to Newcastle, Bundaberg, Port Macquarie, Coffs Harbour, Maryborough, Gladstone, Rockhampton, Townsville and Cairns as well as Grafton, Manly, Hobart, Kiama and Melbourne. Ex-service organisations, service clubs, cubs and girl guides also used her for a variety of functions. Unfortunately, due to the poor state of her hull she was unable to accept an invitation to travel the vast distance back to Exmouth in May 1980.

Numerous Pittwater locals and visitors recall swimming or paddling out and climbing on board the boat and diving off again at the Church Point mooring during the 1970s. On one occasion a group of male medical students from the University of Sydney 'dumped' several nurses on the boat and left them there for several hours, in what the medical students imagined was a hilarious prank.

Between 1964 and 1981 the *Krait* underwent several major refits, using thousands of hours of unpaid volunteer labour. According to a report written by Captain Bill Cockbill this included two overhauls for the Gardner diesel engine, with parts donated by Knox Schlapp Pty Ltd and Gardner agents Ferrier & Dickinson. Larger fuel tanks were also donated by oil company Amoco and fitted by the Army Water Transport Division at Woolwich in Sydney Harbour.

'The first major engine overhaul after the return of *Krait* from North Borneo took a period of four months of spare-time work,'

Captain Cockbill wrote. 'Full credit for this [1978] job must be given to Skipper Jack McRae of McRae Engineering and Skipper Ron Kitchener, engineer.'

Cockbill also recorded that apart from the major jobs, continuous maintenance was carried out on a weekly and monthly basis. 'The vessel is slipped annually at the Palm Beach slipway and scraped and cleaned, underwater fittings serviced, the hull re-caulked and sealed, rudder checked and other normal repairs effected.'

This work was done over three days using volunteer labour supplied by members of the 'Z' Special Unit Association and the RVCP, with occasional assistance from navy cadets. In his report, Cockbill also noted that as long as the maintenance efforts continued there was no reason why 'she could not be able to carry on as long as care and attention is given to her'.

But he warned that the time was coming when more would need to be done. 'The *Krait* will, in the near future, require to be completely restored if she is to survive for future posterity,' he wrote. '*Krait* is much more than just a little wooden ship. It is not what she is but what she has done to earn herself a place in the history of Australia. She is a floating legend to perpetuate the memory of those who served in her and is a reminder to all Australians of the courage and service given by many in the building of our traditions.'

By the early 1980s it was apparent that the *Krait*'s hull had deteriorated to a dangerous point so a fresh fundraising push was launched. Again, many people gave of their hard-earned savings and in 1982 she was sent north to the Ballina slipway for a major refit.

There she narrowly avoided disaster when she was almost lost crossing the notorious Ballina bar in heavy seas. But fortune smiled on the *Krait* once again and she made it to safe harbour, spending the next several months having her hull almost entirely rebuilt using donated hardwood. The cost of the refurbishment was $170,000.

After participating in the 1982 Brisbane Commonwealth Games, the *Krait* returned to Sydney where she was moored at HMAS *Penguin* at Balmoral while her future role was discussed.

* * *

Meanwhile, the debate about the vessel's long-term future was heating up at government level. When, under pressure, the AWM agreed to accommodate the *Krait* in Canberra a public backlash erupted. Many angry donors claimed they had given money to keep the vessel in the water in Sydney – not in a box in Canberra.

In June 1983, under the heading 'Dry display for old spy ship angers sailors' Sydney's *Daily Telegraph* reported: 'Seafarers are up in arms over the committal of the wartime spy ship the *Krait* to a "landlubber museum".'

Angry letters poured into newspapers and one writer under the headline 'Krait's Sad Fate' railed: 'There is nothing so sad and neglected as a ship out of water. With the best will in the world the management of the National War Memorial in Canberra will not be able to sustain life in the *Krait* if she is allowed to die on dry land.'

As the arguments waxed and waned, and after the resignation of Bill Cockbill as her master in December 1983, the RVCP continued to use her for occasional safe-boating courses and the AWM used her for guest cruises around the harbour.

In December 1985, after years of lobbying by the 'Z' Special Unit Association and others, the AWM finally agreed to take official ownership of the *Krait*.

Due to the death of the earlier trustees, three new trustees, Horace Young, John Gardner and Raymond Irish, had been appointed. They handed the *Krait* over to the AWM along with a $50,000 maintenance fund.

The vesting deed, signed by then memorial director James Flemming, clearly states that the $50,000 would be held in a separate bank account and the capital would be used for the 'restoration of the vessel as near as practicable to its operational condition during the Second World War'. Any income would be used for 'maintenance and operating costs of the vessel', it states.

In September 1986, the *Krait* was placed on loan with what would become the ANMM and moved to its then base at Birkenhead Point in Drummoyne.

The loan agreement states that the museum would, 'use the vessel in a skilful and proper manner and at its own expense keep the vessel in good repair and condition'.

It also committed the maritime museum to restoring the vessel as closely as possible to the 'external Jaywick' configuration, in accordance with guidelines provided by the AWM and at the expense of the maritime museum.

It went on to say that, 'If any equipment necessary for operation of the vessel (such as radios, life jackets etc) requires replacement during the term of the agreement, NMM shall obtain and install promptly in the vessel a suitable replacement at NMM expense.'

Of course, if any loss or damage was suffered during the term of the agreement then it would also be covered at the ANMM's expense.

In January 1988, the AWM's head of conservation JA Edwards noted some of the sensitivities associated with the *Krait* in a report to the ANMM's directors. The ANMM's staff requested training runs prior to taking over as crew for the vessel, 'to ensure there was no chance of any difficulties considering that publicity may be involved and the likely load of instant criticism from the old RVCP members previously associated with MV *Krait* if the opportunity arose,' Edwards wrote.

In December 1988, the AWM announced that the *Krait* would be placed on permanent loan with the ANMM and would become one of the ANMM's key floating exhibits when it opened at its new headquarters in Darling Harbour in late 1991.

For this display she was painted in her wartime guise and was as close as she had been since 1945 to looking like the boat that had gone further behind enemy lines than any other.

Although as early as 1985 the AWM had expressed the view that the *Krait* should be restored to her wartime configuration as soon as possible, despite the best efforts of many people during the following 33 years that goal would not be fully realised until 2018.

A keen sailor who has competed in eight Sydney to Hobart Yacht Races and numerous overseas events including the Fastnet Race in the UK, John Nobbs has fond memories of the *Krait* under his father's command in the RVCP, and the boat played an important role in his own life.

As the son of Harold Nobbs, he was intimately involved with the vessel during his younger years and even worked on her when she was slipped at Goddard's slipway in Palm Beach.

These days John and his wife, Francene, divide their time between their homes in Huskisson in Jervis Bay, 183 kilometres south of Sydney, and Antigua in the Bahamas, where they run yacht races and regattas. The couple was married on board the *Krait* at Church Point in Pittwater on a sunny Wednesday, 4 October 1972 and to the best of their knowledge they remain the only people to be wed on the heroic and historic vessel.

Able Seaman, 'Z' Special Unit and Operation Jaywick operative Moss Berryman as a fresh-faced 18-year-old sailor in 1943. He had hoped to be posted to a nice big warship but landed on the little wooden *Krait* after volunteering for special duty. *PHOTO COURTESY MOSS BERRYMAN.*

Moss Berryman, aged 94, at home in Adelaide in 2017. Mr Berryman is the only living survivor of Operation Jaywick. *PHOTO © JAMES ELSBY.*

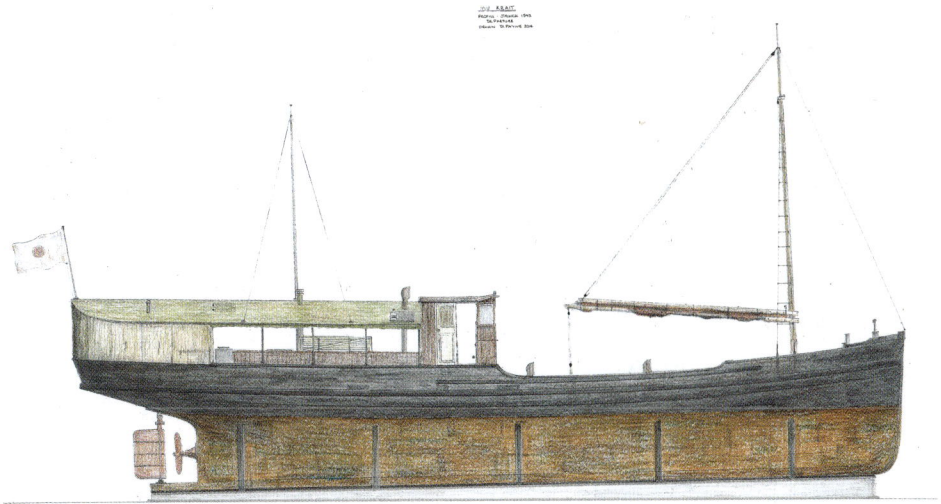

A lovely 2014 drawing of the MV *Krait* in her 1943 livery, by naval architect and National Maritime Museum's curator of historic vessels, David Payne. Note the Japanese flag at the stern, a reminder that the *Krait* was operating under cover. *IMAGE COURTESY DAVID PAYNE.*

A rare portrait, taken at Camp X on the Hawkesbury River, of World War I veteran and master mariner Captain William Roy Reynolds. The original skipper of the *Krait*, he planned the daring raid on Singapore with Major Ivan Lyon.
PHOTO AWM P01806_006.

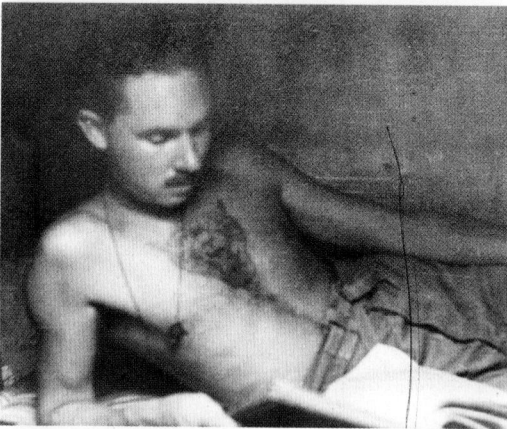

The unconventional Major Ivan Lyon DSC relaxes with a book prior to the Jaywick raid. His tiger head or *rimau* tattoo features prominently on his chest.
PHOTO AWM 045422.

The tidy and elaborate Camp X training camp, built by the Jaywick operatives in a clearing above Refuge Bay on the lower Hawkesbury River. *PHOTO AWM P01806_009.*

A folboat folding canoe like those used by the Jaywick raiders. While camped at the Hawkesbury, the men became expert at assembling the canoes and paddling long distances in a variety of sea states. The ungainly craft carried loads of more than 300 kgs for the outlandish mission.

A fuzzy WWII image of the 'Z' Experimental Station or 'house on the hill' – a top-secret military training camp – in Cairns. Operatives from throughout Australia, Asia and the Pacific trained for unconventional missions at the property. *PHOTO COURTESY BRIAN YOUNG.*

The United States Navy submarine repair ship USS *Chanticleer*, which was based at the Potshot base at Exmouth in 1943. She provided crucial repairs for the *Krait* and luxury digs, whisky and food including ice cream for the Jaywick operatives before they set off for Singapore. *PHOTO US NAVY.*

Operation Jaywick operatives apply the dreaded dye, provided by the cosmetics company Helena Rubinstein, all over their bodies on board MV *Krait* on approach to enemy-held waters and the Lombok Strait. *PHOTO AWM 067336.*

Looking more like holidaymakers than commandos on a dangerous mission in this photo taken by Donald Davidson, Jaywick raiders Ivan Lyon, Andrew 'Happy' Huston, Bob Page, Wally 'Poppa' Falls and Arthur 'Joe' Jones enjoy a refreshing dip on their way into Singapore Harbour. *PHOTO AWM 067337.*

The islands in Singapore Strait are shown in this photo taken by the raiding party, looking towards the harbour from Subar Island, where they rested and identified targets before launching their attack following an exhausting paddle through enemy waters. *PHOTO AWM 067339.*

Donald Davidson's accurate drawing of the Japanese warship that steamed alongside the *Krait* in Lombok Strait during her return journey to Australia. This was one of the rare moments when the Jaywick operatives considered using their high explosives and cyanide tablets.
IMAGE COURTESY BRIAN YOUNG.

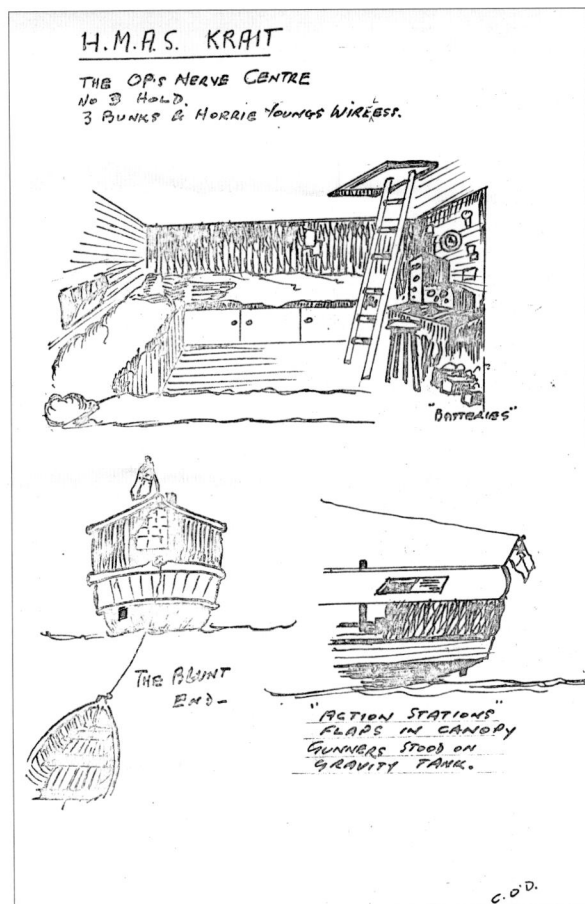

Hand drawings of the *Krait*, including Horrie Young's radio room, which doubled as the officers' quarters and operations room. Sketched in Darwin in 1945 by 'Z' Special operative C.J. O'Dwyer.
IMAGE COURTESY BRIAN YOUNG.

The Operation Jaywick team, photographed in Brisbane following the mission. Back row left to right: Moss Berryman, Fred 'Boof' Marsh, Arthur 'Joe' Jones, Andrew 'Happy' Huston. Middle row left to right: Andy 'Pancake' Crilly, Kevin 'Cobber' Cain, James 'Paddy' McDowell, Horrie Young, Wally 'Poppa' Falls, Ron 'Taffy' Morris. Front row left to right: Ted Carse, Donald Davidson, Ivan Lyon, Jock Campbell and Bob Page. *PHOTO AWM 045424.*

Lieutenant Ted Carse enjoys the drink he dreamed of during the long days at sea on Operation Jaywick – a cold beer. *PHOTO AWM 045406.*

Leading Telegraphist Horrie Young in his formal kit during the post Operation Jaywick celebrations in Brisbane in late 1943. *PHOTO AWM 045415.*

Jaywick members (left to right) Able Seaman Wally 'Poppa' Falls, Lieutenant Donald Davidson, Able Seaman Andrew 'Happy' Huston, Major Ivan Lyon, Able Seaman Arthur 'Joe' Jones and Lieutenant Bob Page raise a glass in Brisbane following their historic mission against Singapore Harbour. PHOTO AWM 134349.

A young, smiling Welsh Corporal Ron 'Taffy' Morris in Brisbane following the Jaywick raid. PHOTO COURTESY BRIAN YOUNG.

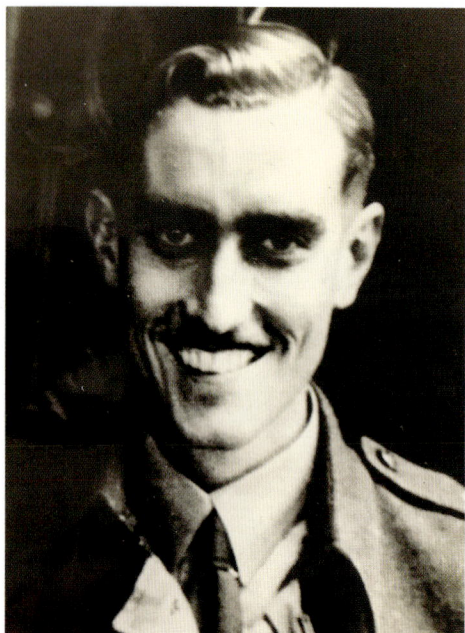

ABOVE LEFT: A very happy Captain Robert Page, photographed in Brisbane after the successful Jaywick mission. He had just wed his sweetheart Roma. He was captured and executed by the Japanese in Singapore in 1945, just weeks before the war ended. *PHOTO COURTESY BRIAN YOUNG.*

ABOVE RIGHT: The headstone of Captain Robert Page in the Kranji War Cemetery, Singapore. *PHOTO COURTESY BRIAN YOUNG.*

LEFT: A rare photograph of the MV *Krait* under sail in an unknown location, probably during her service in 1944 and 1945 with the Darwin-based 'Lugger Maintenance Section' – a code name for 'Z' Special Unit's wartime fleet of specialised vessels. *PHOTO COURTESY JIM CHRISTODOULOU.*

ABOVE: HMAS *Krait* lies alongside at Ambon in September 1945 as an AIF guard of honour awaits the arrival of General Sir Thomas Blamey to take Japan's official surrender. Her history made her the ideal craft for the ceremonial role and she was later used to transport Japanese prisoners between the islands. *PHOTO AWM P00365_004.*

LEFT: Corporal Andy 'Pancake' Crilly in dress uniform during WWII. Like many others, the war took its toll on Crilly in later years, and his family spent many weekends visiting him at the Greenslopes Repatriation General Hospital in Brisbane. *PHOTO COURTESY CRILLY FAMILY.*

BELOW: Corporal 'Pancake' Andy Crilly's wife Patricia with their children Anthony (a future commando himself), Margaret, Ann, Carmel and Andrew Jnr, with the *Krait* in Brisbane before her departure for Sydney in April 1964. *PHOTO COURTESY CRILLY FAMILY.*

MV *Krait* was the star attraction at Farm Cove on Sydney Harbour on Anzac Day 1964 when she was declared a floating memorial by then NSW Governor Sir Eric Woodward. Dozens of spectator craft escorted her up the harbour and thousands of people lined the foreshore. *PHOTO NATIONAL ARCHIVES OF AUSTRALIA.*

Buglers play the *Last Post* during the *Krait* dedication service in Sydney Harbour on Anzac Day 1964, in the presence of Jaywick veterans Moss Berryman, Horrie Young, Arthur 'Joe' Jones and Ted Carse, with the *Krait*'s skipper, Harold Nobbs from the Royal Volunteer Coastal Patrol. *PHOTO NATIONAL ARCHIVES OF AUSTRALIA.*

John and Francene Nobbs with their family after their wedding ceremony on board the *Krait* in Pittwater in 1972. The boat's then skipper, John's dad Harold Nobbs, is far right. *PHOTO COURTESY JOHN AND FRANCENE NOBBS.*

ABOVE: The MV *Krait* in her Royal Volunteer Coastal Patrol livery on the Hawkesbury River north of Sydney in the 1980s. She was a familiar sight around Broken Bay and Pittwater during this period, used widely as a training vessel. *PHOTO COURTESY BRIAN YOUNG.*

LEFT: Taffy Morris, Horrie Young and Joe Jones at Horrie's home in Woy Woy, NSW, in the early 1980s, when they appeared on TV's *This Is Your Life* program about the *Krait*. The men are holding the jungle parang or machete carried on the Operation Jaywick by Young. His son, Brian Young, who was born on the day *Krait* left Australia in 1943, owns the parang today. *PHOTO COURTESY BRIAN YOUNG.*

BOTTOM LEFT: The *Krait* crosses the treacherous Ballina bar in rough seas en route to her 1982 refurbishment at the Ballina Shipyard. *PHOTO WARREN CROSER, COURTESY NORTHERN STAR.*

Rotting hull timbers exposed and replaced during MV *Krait*'s fourteen-month refurbishment at the Bartley Slipway, Woolwich, Sydney Harbour, 2017–18. *PHOTO © JOSH PURNELL.*

Rotting timbers removed from MV *Krait* are stacked near the refurbished stern of the vessel. *PHOTO © JOSH PURNELL.*

Shipwright Brendan Jenkins is a picture of concentration as he fits a brand-new, solid teak plank into the hull of MV *Krait* during her refurbishment. *PHOTO © IAN MCPHEDRAN.*

Shipwright William Olsen uses the ancient method of caulking with a mallet to seal the hull planks of MV *Krait*.

PHOTO © JOSH PURNELL.

Shipwright Andrew Stephenson uses a special tool called a caulking mallet to seal the hull planks on MV *Krait*.

PHOTO © JOSH PURNELL.

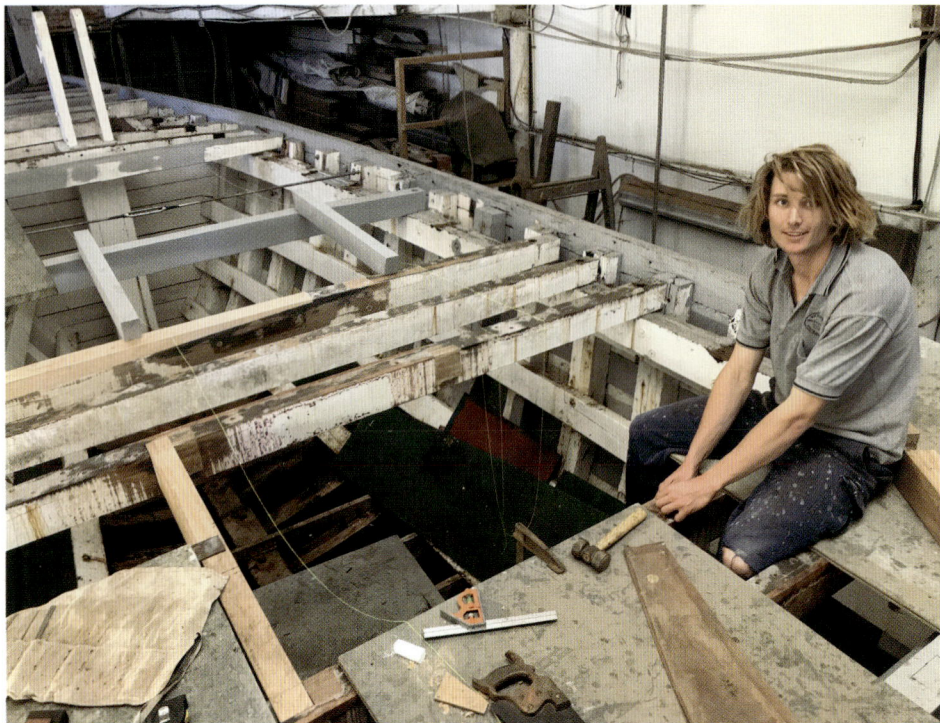

Shipwright Andrew Stephenson repairing the deck and hatches of MV *Krait* during her 2017 refurbishment. *PHOTO © JOSH PURNELL.*

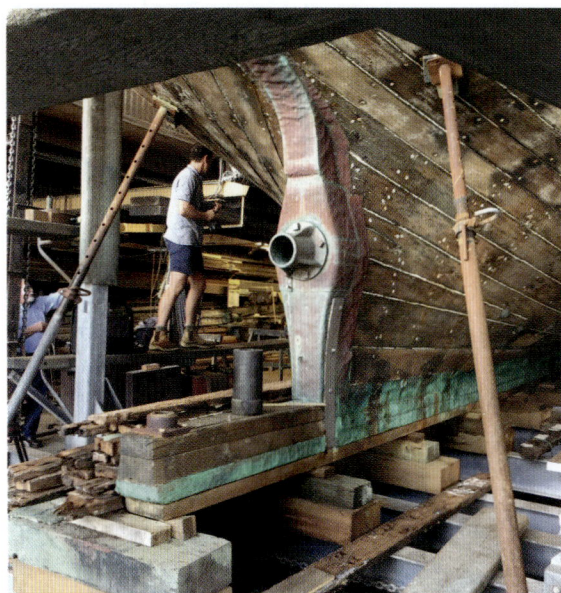

The renovated stern of MV *Krait* as she nears the end of her refurbishment, on the blocks at the Bartley slipway in Woolwich. *PHOTO © IAN MCPHEDRAN.*

Master shipwright Michael 'Wal' Bartley emerges from one of the newly built hatches onto the deck of MV *Krait* during her refurbishment at his Woolwich slipway. *PHOTO © IAN MCPHEDRAN.*

MV *Krait* emerges from the Bartley slipway in Woolwich on 1 March 2018, after spending 14 months high and dry, undergoing a major refurbishment. PHOTO © IAN MCPHEDRAN.

Back in the water at last. MV *Krait* looks as good as new, tied to the wharf after coming off the Bartley slipway in Woolwich. PHOTO © IAN MCPHEDRAN.

World War II 'Z' Special Unit veteran and prime mover behind the *Krait* preservation project, Douglas Herps, with the vessel at the Maritime Museum prior to his death in April 2015. Douglas spent years lobbying for the preservation of the vessel, which he regarded as a fitting memorial to his mates. PHOTO ROHAN KELLY NEWSPIX.

An artist's rendering of the proposed MV *Krait* display at the end of Wharf Seven at the Australian National Maritime Museum in Darling Harbour, Sydney. The *Krait* can be seen in the glass box at top left and will be the star attraction at the museum's proposed new Maritime Heritage Precinct. IMAGE COURTESY NATIONAL MARITIME MUSEUM.

Marine surveyor the late Warwick Thomson (far left) explains the MV *Krait* refurbishment to (left to right) National Maritime Museum Council chair Peter Dexter, museum director Kevin Sumption and businessman Michael Chaney at the Bartley slipway in Woolwich in 2017. Sadly, Mr Thomson, who played a crucial role in the vessel's restoration, passed away before the job was finished. PHOTO COURTESY NATIONAL MARITIME MUSEUM.

Unfortunately, the Gardner diesel engine was not working at the time, so the 60 wedding guests had to be towed on board the *Krait* to an anchorage in Towlers Bay, just across the headland from the old Camp X at Refuge Bay, where the bride and groom both boarded the boat from sailing vessels – with the bride even having a water police escort. The ceremony took place in the bow and the reception was a smorgasbord set up on top of the engine room hatch.

'I remember Lou d'Alpuget wanted to write it up in the paper to get more publicity for the vessel and he was told, "No, this is very private, people are donating money and they don't want the vessel to be used like that." So it … wasn't given any publicity and it was a one-off,' Francene recalled.

John admits that in his younger days he didn't really think about the history and about how special the *Krait* actually was to Australia.

'I must confess and say it's only as I'm growing older now that I really come to grips with what she did and how well she's lasted,' he said. He has been around boats all his life and in the 1980s the couple moved overseas to sail yachts for wealthy owners in places such as the UK, Mediterranean, the USA, Canada and the Caribbean.

'I've been in boats all over the world and the owners often say that they are not really the owners but only the custodians of some fine vessels,' John said. 'That's brilliant and I feel the same way about the *Krait* now.'

While there is general agreement that the *Krait* was built in Japan, John Nobbs suggested that she might have been built in Java: 'Some of the old guys up at Goddard's, the old chippies, took one look at her and said, "Well, it was built by two families." Family A on the portside and family B on the starboard side because she's not symmetrical. She's not identical side for side: her frames and scantlings aren't the same; there are differences. That method of building was very much a Javanese thing. Built on the beach, the family living down there built that side and the family living on that side built that side and that's all that was about it as a fishing boat.'

John comes from a strong family tradition of service. His father, Harold, was awarded an MBE for his service to the RVCP and his grandfather, Henry Nobbs, was awarded an OBE for his service to the blind. He had lost his sight to a German bullet as a young British soldier on the Somme in World War I and came to Australia after the war to open a new factory for Holbrooks Ltd. After World War I he helped to establish Sydney Legacy and he also founded the NSW Blinded Soldiers Association.

During his time working on the *Krait* at the Palm Beach slipway, John Nobbs was extremely impressed by her six-cylinder Gardner diesel engine that was fitted in Cairns before the Jaywick raid.

Seventy-five years later, the old diesel runs with the same reliable 'clackety, clackety, clack, clack, clack'.

16

In memoriam

Although the extraordinary, secret story of Operation Jaywick had been mentioned briefly in newspaper reports in August 1945, the government did not publicly acknowledge the mission in any detail until 1946.

During the first official statement to the House of Representatives in Canberra on 1 August 1946 concerning Operation Jaywick, the Minister for the Army, Frank Forde, at first declined to name the operatives who had conducted the mission.

According to the Melbourne *Herald*, the first woman elected to the House of Representatives and Australia's first female cabinet minister, Dame Enid Lyons, interjected insisting that the men be named and recorded in Hansard. Some reports suggested that Dame Enid had earlier recommended that the six Jaywick canoe raiders should be awarded the VC.

So Forde duly read out the names of the 14 operatives and their awards, and outlined the mission and the men's 'outstanding bravery and devotion to duty under circumstances of extreme hazard'.

'They reached Australia without loss or mishap on the 19th of October 1943, having spent over 40 days in enemy occupied and controlled areas under conditions of constant strain and danger and having carried out a highly successful and crippling attack on the enemy, concerning the methods of which the Japanese are still in the dark,' the minister said.

Numerous newspapers then carried reports about Operation Jaywick, including Andy Crilly's hometown paper, *The Queensland Times*, under the headline 'Ipswich Soldier's Part in "Hush Hush" Blow at Japs'.

'I was just one of the lucky ones in having an opportunity to go,' he told the paper. 'I know there were hundreds of others who would have been in it.'

The government's announcement in Parliament in 1946 was, shockingly, also the first official news that Bob Page's wife, Roma, received about her husband's terrible fate in Operation Rimau.

In 2013 I visited Mrs Page at her tidy unit in Canberra for a chat and a cup of tea. Her home was a mini-shrine to her late husband and alongside the photos of the happy couple on their wedding day was a print of the famous and dramatic painting by Dennis Adams that portrays Bob Page and Joe Jones attaching a limpet mine to a Japanese ship in Singapore harbour during Operation Jaywick. The original painting hangs in the AWM.

Despite her then 91 years, Mrs Page was as sharp as a tack and she was still bitter that the army had never provided her with a proper explanation or even an official notification about Bob's death. She had remarried after the war but it did not work out and she reverted to her first married name of Page. Even though she and Bob had only spent a few short wartime weeks together as a married couple, she carried her love of him until the end.

'Well, I only have to read the letters and it's, it's all there,' she later told ABC TV's *Australian Story* for its feature on the *Krait*. 'And I cry and cry and cry. It's such an incredible love I had for that man. There's been something there all along that has taken a hold of me.'

The only official notice she had received about his fate was a telegram in November 1945 that had said he had died from illness in a prison camp.

'When I read about the executions, I felt numb,' she told me. 'I still haven't been officially informed about what happened to Bob.'

Mrs Page also told ABC TV that the *Krait* was 'very precious' to her. 'I think it's a wonderful little ship to have done all the things it did, travelled all those miles.'

Her anger about the lack of information regarding Bob's fate was somewhat appeased on 1 November 2013 when she was guest of honour at the Last Post Ceremony at the AWM that was dedicated to the memory of Captain Robert Charles Page, DSO.

'The service really only lasted about five minutes, but it was just so beautiful. I had two little roses, rosebuds and some lily of the valley that had been on my wedding cake. And so I took those with me and we put them in amongst the flowers I had.'

Bob Page's courage has been an inspiration to following generations and not just to soldiers. Mrs Page received a letter penned more than 50 years after the war by a Singapore resident called Noraini Nain Sardi, who had no personal connection to the story but had finally found his grave after a year of searching: 'For the past four years I have been visiting him [Bob] and the rest of the "Z" Special Unit at least three times a year,' Ms Sardi wrote. 'I've always wondered if I would ever get the chance to speak to you. I know this doesn't make sense at all. But I wanted to tell you that I think Bob Page was a wonderful man. I found out that you were here seven months ago. I saw the poppy flowers that you and your sister placed on his grave. I wish I had been there a day earlier. I'm glad that after all these years of hoping and waiting, I'm finally able to express how I feel about Bob. I'm sorry if I have caused any inconvenience to you with this letter. I hope you'll take very good care of yourself. I'll continue to visit Bob and his friends in Kranji [War Cemetery] for as long as I live. By the way, I am getting married this November to someone I'm very much in love with. I just thought I'd share some of my happiness with you.'

Roma Page died in Canberra in October 2016 aged 95.

* * *

In the decades after 1946, numerous unofficial memorials, plaques and monuments to the *Krait* and Operation Jaywick were erected between Australia's east coast and Singapore Island.

These include most of the significant places in the story of the *Krait*'s amazing journey – Refuge Bay on the Hawkesbury River, Exmouth in Western Australia, Sentosa in Singapore, and Hervey Bay and Cairns in Queensland as well as the SRD Memorial at HMAS *Stirling*, Garden Island near Perth, where the Rimau operatives, including the Jaywick six, trained for their doomed mission.

The memorial includes an honour roll featuring the names of scores of special forces operatives killed during dozens of classified operations that remained top secret for decades and the inscription:

170

Erected in memory of the members of Services Reconnaissance
Department who gave their lives for King and country in the
Pacific campaign during World War II.
   LEST WE FORGET.

These operations were run by either the British SOE or the
Australian SRD, the forerunner of SOA. Some early Australian-
run operations were conducted under the umbrella of SOE
Australia.

While Operation Jaywick was a magnificent, if underplayed,
success story, many of the hundreds of missions conducted by
Australia's secret troops throughout the Southwest Pacific between
1942 and 1945 were failures.

At Refuge Bay, a metal plaque carrying the 'Z' Special Unit
emblem and attached to a sandstone boulder reads simply:

Z Special Unit commandos sailed from Refuge Bay in MV *Krait*
to attack enemy shipping in Singapore harbour on 26 September
1943. Operation Jaywick was considered to be the most daring
and successful seaborne raid in military history.

The cairn at Learmonth, built near where the raiders departed
from Australia, features a bronze plaque with the legend:

Krait departed for Singapore from this spot on Operation Jaywick
September 2, 1943. Vessel returned on October 19, 1943 having
sunk 37,000 tons of enemy shipping. Erected by 'Z' Special Unit
International (Inc) 2 September, 1993.

At the cenotaph in Cairns, another memorial plaque is dedicated ...

In memory of the heroes of M and Z special commando units who trained on this site and the gallant ship *Krait*.

AWM director Brendan Nelson believes that the *Krait* is precisely the sort of wartime artefact that the creator of the AWM, war correspondent, author and historian Charles Bean, had in mind when he revealed his vision for a national shrine to house a collection that would honour the sacrifice of so many young Australians following the horrors that he witnessed at Gallipoli and on the Western Front during World War I: 'If you go back to the very start, [Bean] knew that in order for them to be remembered, he would have to collect objects and relics; these really sacred artefacts, repositories of memory, of heroism, of courage, and the good and the bad, the great and the small.'

In the annals of Australians at war, he went on to say, the Jaywick raid stands out for many reasons: 'You've got to have the imaginative capacity to think how Australians were thinking in 1942 and in 1943. [The year] 1942 was our most important after 1788. Our vital interests were at stake. Australians had every reason to believe that we were at real risk of invasion by the Japanese. We now know in hindsight they had no real plans but they certainly directly attacked Australia [and her territories] 100 times – midget submarines in Sydney Harbour and of course the bombing of Darwin [and the northwest], the Kokoda Campaign and Milne Bay, Buna-Gona, Sananada and so on.'

Nelson drew comparisons between the epic nature of the 7000-kilometre journey of the *Krait* and the raid on Singapore with Captain Cook's feat in reaching Botany Bay: 'Sometimes we look at HMS Bark *Endeavour* and the replica of it and think, "My goodness, Cook and his crew sailed all the way over here at a time when a quarter of them were sinking",' he said. 'But here, these 14 men get in this little boat and go up to an island near Singapore and then six of them in these little folding canoe boats, paddle an over 100-kilometre return trip, travelling at night, to put limpet mines on Japanese ships in the middle of Singapore harbour – daring is probably not sufficient a description of it.'

He added that the fact the Sydney Harbour foreshore was surrounded by so many well-wishers when the *Krait* motored in on Anzac Day in 1964 spoke volumes about the importance of the modest fishing boat and its story.

Moss Berryman said he'd read reports that there were more spectator craft following the *Krait* than had followed the royal yacht *Britannia* with the Queen on board several years before.

'The harbour was full of boats, big and small, and we had this escort right down the harbour to Farm Cove. What a sight that was to see all these boats,' Berryman marvelled.

The value of the *Krait*, according to Brendan Nelson, lies in the fact that people can see and touch it and imagine what it might have been like for the men during Operation Jaywick.

'This was not going on a nice little cruise around Sydney Harbour, but to get in that boat and go all the way up to Southeast Asia, up to Singapore and to do that knowing that any moment you could be challenged … And if you were killed instantly you would regard that as being fortunate because most likely you'd be tortured before being killed. And that they did that, then came back to Australia, and having done this extraordinary feat they couldn't even tell anybody.

'It was extraordinary courage every second, every hour of their day was courage and yet they couldn't tell anybody, couldn't tell their families, wives – the nation had no idea and yet it had a significant unsettling impact on the Japanese.'

Nelson believes that Jaywick speaks to the character of the 14 men involved. 'And that is why the *Krait* is so important. It tells their story.'

War relics such as the *Krait* act not only as reminders of the courage and sacrifice of mankind, he said, but they can also inspire future generations. 'I asked an 11-year-old what one of our exhibitions meant to him and he replied, "I now know they were real people and they weren't made up." That's what this is about – they know it's real.'

The debate about whether old boats should be kept in the water or removed and preserved under climate-controlled conditions, in expensive indoor facilities, is a hot topic at the AWMM and at other museums and boatyards around the world.

The long-term preservation of timber artefacts can only be assured indoors under controlled conditions, but the intrinsic value of a boat is in her ability to float, bobbing up and down with the motion of waves and currents. Timber that lies under the waterline is almost naturally preserved but anything exposed above the waterline is subject to degradation from rainwater and the environment.

The earlier push to move the *Krait* to an indoor display area at the AWM in Canberra, that had so divided the *Krait* 'community' and the wider public who had supported fundraising campaigns to keep her afloat, had seen battlelines drawn up.

The *Krait* had remained displayed at Birkenhead Point at Drummoyne on Sydney Harbour pending a decision. Estimates at the time put the cost of building a climate-controlled facility in Canberra at a very conservative $1.4 million and that did not include the cost of transporting her from Sydney to the nation's capital.

After the AWM's decision in 1988 to hand her on permanent loan to the maritime museum, where she was to be kept afloat, the debate died down and the out-of-the-water faction conceded defeat to those who wanted her kept afloat. It would be more than 20 years and due largely to the efforts of Douglas Herps that the discussion about the boat's future would return to centre stage.

In 2014 the AWM's position was clearly articulated in a letter from senior staffer Major General (retired) Brian Dawson to Herps: 'The vessel should be removed from the water and exhibited in a shore-based facility. For the vessel to remain in Sydney it should be in an on-shore facility with environmental and humidity control. Modern curatorial solutions should be used to enable visitors to understand its story and its significance. It should be displayed in its fully intact form rather than partially deconstructed.'

ANMM council member and ex-NSW Liberal Party leader Peter Collins is adamant that the *Krait* should be the centrepiece of a display focused exclusively on special forces. '*Krait* will be the magnet for anyone with an interest in special forces. It almost invites the broadening of the special forces collection of the museum.'

Because so much of the historical material about Australian special forces operations is owned by the units and therefore displayed out of public reach at private museums inside the SAS headquarters at Swanbourne near Perth and Commando HQ at Holsworthy near Sydney, the *Krait* project presents an opportunity for the general public to gain access to some unique Australian military history.

'As a former Honorary Colonel, First Commando Regiment, and a then-serving Senior Naval Officer, I couldn't even get access to the SAS Museum in Swanbourne when I was last in

Perth, because it was too hard,' Collins said. 'With some of our historical collections on defence bases, we need to accept that it is too hard. That may be the repository; it may be where you store material, but in order to display material somewhere where you'll get the kind of national and international visitation that you need for a cultural institution, the best place to do that is the national maritime museum.'

17

In their footsteps

The hallowed status of the Jaywick and Rimau operations have inspired a number of Australian soldiers to attempt to follow the path of the World War II operatives by re-enacting the missions.

In 1971, Bob Lowry, a young Australian Army lieutenant, led a group of nine men from 108 Field Battery on a 12-day paddle along the Jaywick route. The party included four two-man canoes and a support vessel. The aim was to visit as many as possible of the island hideouts used by both the Jaywick and Rimau operatives, as well as the refugees from Singapore who fled the invading Japanese in 1942.

Lowry wrote about his mission in the January 1972 edition of the *Australian Army Journal*. When the troops paddled onto Merapas Island, where the Rimau raiders had planned to rendezvous with the submarine, they met a local man named Karta who claimed to have helped with the burial of two of the raiders who had been killed on the island by the Japanese, when he was a boy of 10.

Lowry wrote: 'He said that he had seen three of the raiders and been to their camp to talk to them. One day twelve Japanese had come in two boats, landed on the northern shore and engaged in a skirmish with the three raiders, who had only pistols. Two of the raiders were killed while the third escaped in a rubber canoe. The raiders killed the Japanese captain.'

Karta even took Lowry and his team to the place where the operatives were supposedly buried near a stone sangar or mini-fortress (lying up place in modern parlance) that was the site of their last stand. A rudimentary dig was undertaken but they could not find any sign of human remains.

However, the body of one of the missing operatives, a young Scottish naval officer called Gregor Riggs, was eventually found on Merapas Island in 1994 and was re-interred at Kranji War Cemetery in Singapore, along with the partial remains of the Australian commando killed with him, Colin Cameron.

Three canoes and six of the eight paddlers who set out on Lowry's 1971 re-enactment mission arrived at Changi Yacht Club at 10.15 am on 19 September 1971.

'As a result of the exercise those taking part have a greater understanding and appreciation of the difficulties that confronted the raiders,' he wrote.

In 1994 then SAS Major Jim Truscott decided to mark the fiftieth anniversary of the compromised Rimau raid by retracing the escape route taken by most of the doomed operators.

That first ever Operation Rimau re-enactment, called 'Rimau Retrace', was only able to take place because the commanding officer of special forces at the time, Brigadier Jim Wallace, took the decision to allow the journey to proceed without the required 'safety boat' that was mandated under Occupational Health and Safety provisions for any venture operating more than 400 metres from the shore. Truscott believes that the reason Operation Rimau had never been re-enacted until then was because of its status as a 'failure'. He set out to remedy this.

Jaywick, on the other hand, had already been re-enacted and was the focus of commemorative services at Kranji War Cemetery in Singapore on 26 September every year.

Wallace ticked off on the operation on the proviso that Truscott, who was serving on secondment with the Pilbara Regiment at the time, carried a satellite phone so that he could call in to his 'safety officer' – another former SAS officer, Rick Moor – who was based in Canberra. In those days, global phones came in a large suitcase to store their cumbersome antenna.

The Truscott re-enactment involved three Klepper canvas folboats similar to the canoes used for the Jaywick raid, with two men paddling in each boat. There were four commandos, another soldier from the Pilbara Regiment and Truscott.

The canoes retraced the route of the majority of the fleeing operatives to Singkep Island where many of the men were either killed or captured in October 1944.

'We did a huge amount of research to locate the route and of course on a few occasions the route was the same as where some of the Jaywick guys had gone as well. So, we visited some Jaywick locations just by sheer coincidence. But, as close as possible, we followed the route from when the *Mustika* [the mothership that the Rimau operatives had hijacked] was blown up,' Truscott said. 'When the *Mustika* was blown up, they paddled off and they were towing rubber rafts full of explosives. Lyon [who had blown up the *Mustika*] had not given up. He was a determined man, Lyon.'

When Truscott and his team arrived on Merapas Island southeast of Singapore they found that the rock sangar or mini-fortress, that had been built by the survivors and seen by Bob Lowry in 1971, was still standing. The sangar was built to the height of a man from coastal rocks carried inland by the Rimau operatives. Truscott's team also found several badly corroded limpet mines on the island.

Merapas was the rendezvous point for the Rimau operatives with their pick-up submarine that never came and 18 of them – including the Jaywick survivors Bob Page, Wally Falls and Boof Marsh – had waited there in vain before splitting up following an enemy assault.

Two of the operatives, Gregor Riggs and Colin Cameron, were killed by the Japanese on Merapas not far from the rock sangar. By sheer coincidence the body of Riggs had been exhumed in 1994 just days before Truscott's team arrived at the end of their two-week paddle.

Truscott believes that honouring the feats of Australian soldiers, and especially special forces soldiers, is extremely important. He too strongly supports the concept of a special forces museum built around the *Krait* at the ANMM in Sydney's Darling Harbour. He also feels that Australian special forces have been largely ignored in places such as the AWM, even though a special forces exhibition opened during 2017 has vastly improved recognition of the achievements of the nation's clandestine soldiers.

'It would be great to see a proper display [in Sydney] that might even include the rock sangar that still stands on Merapas Island,' Truscott suggested. 'It would be easy enough to send a boat in to collect the rocks and then re-assemble it back in Australia.'

Mick Donaldson is a highly decorated army veteran who served for 10 years full-time with the SAS. He spent four years as a senior non-commissioned officer and patrol commander with deployments to Iraq, Afghanistan, East Timor and the Solomon Islands, among others, and remains a reservist with the regiment. Donaldson was at the 'tip of the spear' during the 2003 US-led invasion of Iraq when the Australian SAS roamed the western desert searching for enemy missile launchers.

These days he runs a tour company called The Adventure Group or 'TAG', running tours to battlefields including Kokoda, Iraq, North Africa, Malta and the Western Front, employing mainly ex-regiment soldiers whom he knows and trusts.

'We do what others can't or what others won't, as well as putting a unique spin on some old favourites such as Kokoda,' he told me. 'For example, when we do Kokoda we talk about what it is like to be in a few gunfights. Around the camp fire we may or may not tell a few war stories.'

After leaving the army in 2004 Donaldson joined the British firm AKE that provided high-end security services to media companies such as CNN and Japan's NHK as their staff reported from conflict zones around the globe. He then moved to the United Nations to manage security for UN-supervised elections in Iraq and Afghanistan before joining an American telco based in Dubai providing mobile phone services to the US government across Iraq and the region.

When his two children reached university age, he and his wife, Nicole, decided to move back to Australia and to start their tour company, with one of their key aims being to employ as many former soldiers as possible to prevent them from being forced into the fraught and dangerous business of security contracting.

Philanthropy and veteran support networks are key planks of the TAG business model and to that end Donaldson planned another re-enactment of the Jaywick raid, this time to coincide with the seventy-fifth anniversary of the attack on Singapore in September 2018. The mission was also designed to support existing special forces charities, the SAS Resources Trust and Commando Welfare Trust, that were established to assist the families of wounded or dead operators, and other veterans' charities.

'We are ready to do it, we have got our ducks in a row,' Donaldson said in April 2018. 'It [Jaywick] is an under-told story in our military annals. It's an incredible feat, back when ships were made of wood and men were made of steel. I am in awe of what they achieved and I have done some crazy stuff myself in my time. That admiration and respect will only grow as we step through that re-enactment.'

A military history buff, Donaldson was aware of Operation Jaywick as a youngster and studied the mission in detail after he joined the army. The feats of 'Z' Special Unit and the World War II Independent Commando Companies were revered at SAS headquarters at Swanbourne near Perth and SAS troopers often stood as the guard of honour for the Second/Second Independent Company commemoration service in Kings Park each year. The Second/Second had distinguished itself in Timor during World War II as part of Sparrow Force. There was even high-level chat at one time about changing the name of the SAS to 'Z' Special Unit.

For the seventy-fifth anniversary charity re-enactment Mick Donaldson planned to launch 10 two-man German-designed Klepper folboats to retrace the exact route of the Jaywick raiders into Singapore harbour, arriving in time for the seventy-fifth anniversary ceremony at Kranji War Cemetery on 26 September 2018.

The concept called for each canoe to include a veteran and a fundraiser, or 'fundy', to raise money for the various charities.

They hoped the teams would also include amputees from the Royal Marine's Special Boat Service (SBS) in memory of the British personnel who served on Jaywick.

A special guest in one of the canoes would be army veteran Tony Crilly from Albury in New South Wales, whose father was Andy 'Pancake' Crilly, MM, the cook for the Jaywick mission.

Donaldson's re-enactment team was due to fly into Bali to join the *Krait* replacement or 'mother ship' to carry them through Lombok Strait to Pompong Island – the rear base and pick-up point for the 1943 raid. The vessel would then act as the safety boat for the duration of the journey.

'Once the canoes are launched the safety boat won't come near us unless she has to. She will be over the horizon so we get that sense of isolation,' Donaldson said. 'We plan to camp where the boys camped and we will do some paddling at night just as they did. We are leaving an extra two days to get across from Pompong so we will have five days of paddling all up.'

And would they be carrying limpet mines like their predecessors? 'I don't think the Singaporeans would be too happy with that.'

Donaldson said the team did not have a specific fundraising target but would dearly love to reach a six-figure sum with the help of some corporate players and publicity from a planned documentary film.

'We would like to partner with the war memorial as well,' he said. 'The benefits are massive and I have been overwhelmed by the number of veterans who want to be a part of this.'

18

Controversy and cost

After 30 years spent carting fish and supplies across the South China Sea, refugees around Singapore, commando raiders deep behind enemy lines and timber throughout Borneo, the *Krait* was in need of some tender loving care when she arrived back in Sydney on Anzac Day 1964.

She had undergone minor maintenance work in Brisbane after her long journey from Borneo before cruising south to her new home on Pittwater, but the hard-working timber vessel was beginning to show her age.

Although she was accepted at Farm Cove that day by New South Wales Governor Lieutenant General Sir Eric Woodward on behalf of the people of Australia, the *Krait* has never had 'official' war memorial status.

It was Sir Eric who bestowed the only formal status on her when he said to the service padres present at the handover ceremony: 'Reverend Sirs, we ask that you bid God's blessing on this memorial.' Later in the ceremony, according to the official program, he asked the patron of the RVCP, retired Rear Admiral Herbert Buchanan, 'to accept the vessel in trust to be maintained as a floating war memorial'. That was duly done and the governor unveiled the memorial plaque. The guests of honour at that ceremony were surviving Jaywick operatives Ted Carse, Horrie Young, Joe Jones and Moss Berryman.

However, the *Krait* does not appear on the Australian Government's Register of War Memorials. The only 'official' memorial to the Operation Jaywick and Operation Rimau missions listed on the register is a memorial garden at Point Clare on Brisbane Water near Gosford in New South Wales.

The garden is north of Operation Jaywick's Camp X training camp at Refuge Bay on Cowan Creek, in an area that must have been familiar to the operatives as they trained in their folboat canoes for the mission. It was dedicated on 21 September 2003 to mark the sixtieth anniversary of the raid on Singapore.

'Its location, on a well-used cycling and walking trail, is ideally positioned to help educate the public on the contribution made by RAN personnel to the success of the Jaywick mission and serves as a memorial to those who lost their lives on the ill-fated Rimau raid,' the Register of War Memorials notes.

In a letter to Douglas Herps during a stakeholder consultation in October 2014, the Assistant Director National Collection at the Australian War Memorial, Brian Dawson, wrote that the 'MV *Krait* should be dedicated as a war memorial, which should not inhibit its potential for interpretation'.

As far as veterans of 'Z' Special Unit and other Commando units were concerned there was no doubt that the *Krait* already was a war memorial, as stated on the plaque in her wheelhouse:

MV *Krait* dedicated as a war memorial in the presence of His Excellency the Governor of New South Wales Sir Eric Woodward on Anzac Day 1964. In memory of men of 'Z' Special Unit who lost their lives on special operations 1939–1945.

It also details the operation and lists the names of the men who took the *Krait* to Singapore and back. The wording is slightly misleading because only the army members of the Jaywick team were actually members of 'Z' Special Unit.

In ANMM director Kevin Sumption's view, the *Krait* is the most significant vessel in the museum's floating collection in terms of the stories it tells. 'That's not to underplay the significance of the other vessels; they all have important stories, but … in terms of the national story and the importance of *Krait* and Operation Jaywick and also all the way through to the evacuation of refugees from Singapore to Australia and its career thereafter in Borneo, it's a rich history … it's obviously a floating memorial and it's held in such high regard by commando veterans, special forces veterans and even the SAS, who regularly turn up in large numbers for our November Remembrance Service.'

The retired Oberon-class submarine HMAS *Onslow* is the ANMM's number one drawcard. People of all ages clamour to climb inside the Cold War–era vessel to get a glimpse of life on board a navy submarine. The sub, along with the destroyer HMAS *Vampire* – the sister ship of the HMAS *Voyager* tragically lost in 1964 in a collision with the aircraft carrier HMAS *Melbourne* off Jervis Bay with the loss of 82 souls – and the *Endeavour* replica are the museum's three most prominent vessels in the floating collection.

Sumption, who is originally from Wales and married to an Australian, has been working at the museum on and off since it opened in 1991. He was the inaugural curator of the immigration and US gallery collections. He has also had stints at the Royal Observatory and the National Maritime Museum at Greenwich in London.

'It is in my blood,' he said. 'So the chance to come back here and help with the refocusing and rebuilding of the museum was too good an opportunity to pass up.'

Speaking in his office at Wharf Seven, he said that securing the long-term future of the *Krait* is one of his key objectives. With a view overlooking the vintage lightship *Carpentaria* and with the Sydney CBD reflected in a glassy Darling Harbour beyond, Sumption pointed out that the museum's remit is very broad because it is the national storage for all things maritime.

'We are very focused on not only the defence stories but the immigration stories and importantly also, Indigenous stories; saltwater people stories,' he says. 'In broad terms, those are the three major areas the museum looks at and *Krait* is a very important story, in terms of not just maritime but Australia, Second World War, Special Services, all of those kinds of stories. It also complements the work, particularly with HMAS *Onslow* and the use of our submarine service in the Special Services.'

He agrees with Nelson's comment that the difficulty with telling navy stories is that the objects tend to be so big. 'You need a significant budget to keep a warship open and available to the public. To keep *Krait* floating is a significant and ongoing investment. It's not just preserving it and putting it in a showcase and not having to worry about it. These objects tend to take a lot more care and attention and ultimately money, which makes them particularly difficult, generation to generation, to ensure that they're there and they're doing their storytelling.'

Brendan Nelson also agrees that after the 2017–18 refurbishment and 1943 reconfiguration the *Krait* will be fine to remain in the water with a greatly enhanced dockside display for years. 'But in the longer term, we owe it to ourselves, let alone to them, to actually get it out of the water, have it in a purpose-built facility there right on the water's edge, harbourside at Darling Harbour.'

Nelson suggested that once her long-term future is decided and she is placed in a permanent exhibition out of the water surrounded by the artefacts of the Jaywick men, ownership of the *Krait* should be transferred to the maritime museum. 'There would not be a lot of logic in it continuing to be owned by the Australian War Memorial.'

Stunning architectural plans have been drawn up for a new facility to be built on the end of the museum's Wharf 7. It would feature the *Krait* in a large glass box with an interactive display that would include artefacts used by special forces operatives, to tell the story of Operation Jaywick and other secret missions. Lit up at night, it would be a spectacularly beautiful sight from the water and for the millions of tourists who promenade around Darling Harbour.

But it would not be cheap. Such a project would cost upwards of $20 million and given the challenge of gaining any corporate support for the $1 million-plus 2017–18 refurbishment, any future major outlays would have to come in the main from the federal and New South Wales governments. But it is also hoped that the corporate sector, particularly the dozens of blue chip companies including banks and casinos dotted around Darling Harbour, Pyrmont and Barangaroo, will take up the challenge of preserving the *Krait* and her story.

High-profile businessman Michael Chaney, whose late father, Sir Frederick Chaney, was awarded the Air Force Cross during World War II for a daring rescue mission in Borneo when he piloted one of the Auster aircraft attached to 'Z' Special Unit, is a strong supporter of the *Krait* project. The chairman of Wesfarmers and former chairman of National Australia Bank, who inspected the *Krait* on the slips at Woolwich, said in his view the only way to provide the necessary funds for a proper display was with both government and private sector contributions on the basis of one-third federal government, one-third state government and one-third private sector. If, say, the final cost were in the vicinity of \$15–20 million, that would be between \$5 million and \$6.7 million from each.

'The *Krait* story is remarkable and it deserves to be told, and the boat deserves a proper home,' Chaney said. 'One of the challenges is that there are endless causes. All businesses are beset with requests for donations at all times. I think there would be people who would be potentially supportive of the cause once the story was told. It is a project that ought to happen.'

Peter Collins agrees it would be great for the corporate sector to assist with funding for the *Krait* project, but he feels it is up to the federal government to fill any funding shortfall. He described the *Krait* as a vital Australian story for all times. 'This is part of our fabric. It's also part of the story about where the ADF will go in the future because this was the most dramatic and successful operation undertaken by our embryonic special forces.'

'Special forces', he said, was a relatively modern military concept that really only started in the 1940s. 'But what we now take for granted – and what is the force of choice in virtually any conflict that we've been involved in in the last 20 years – had its origins back in Jaywick, back in those early days with extremely modest resources. And *Krait* is a matchstick boat that really typifies the resourcefulness and ingenuity of those soldiers and sailors who made up the small Jaywick team. We cobbled together our first special forces operation and, in European terms, conducted it at the extreme end of the theatre of operations. It was amazing that it succeeded and that no one was killed.'

A 2016 feasibility study into the *Krait* restoration and display project commissioned by the maritime museum found that most people interviewed had little or no knowledge of the *Krait* and Operation Jaywick, but were very positive once the story had been explained.

The ANMM has traditionally focused on the civilian aspects of the nation's maritime history, but under plans to transfer the Sydney heritage fleet to the museum precinct for permanent display, the military story will be greatly enhanced. Once completed, the northwestern section of the museum will house one of the largest operational heritage fleets in the world.

Nelson and Sumption both regard the heritage display with a focus on the *Krait* and the military aspects of maritime history as perfectly appropriate. Sumption says it's important for the museum to take a balanced view between civilian and military, but he places MV *Krait* in the top 2 per cent of its 140,000 artefacts.

'We've got the Naval Heritage Museum over at Garden Island. We've got the Naval Heritage Centre on Spectacle Island. We've got the two largest in naval history-telling with the submarine and the destroyer and two dedicated galleries. So there's quite a bit of storytelling already given over to the Royal Australian Navy,' he said. 'In amongst all of that, the other maritime heritage stories also need to be told. I don't see that there's any kind of issues with increasing our storytelling; quite the contrary. We don't do enough storytelling around *Krait* and the real challenge for us is to bring *Krait* to life now.'

To that end, the museum is producing a film on the Jaywick raid to screen alongside films about Oberon-class submarines and navy destroyers in the museum's 'action stations' display. The

Assistant Director for Public Engagement and Research, Michael Harvey, says the aim is to explain the history and significance of the *Krait*.

'Then, when visitors see it, it will be more meaningful for them knowing the background in a reasonably dramatic way,' he said. 'It's a relatively inoffensive-looking boat but actually it was responsible for the destruction of a substantial tonnage of Japanese shipping. It was a weapon of war, and so to be able to demonstrate that will make looking at the vessel something that will be really quite memorable.'

Harvey pointed out that the Jaywick story is also very relevant to the history of Singapore: 'We hope that we will be able to work with museums in Singapore to be able to share the story there as well. Whether it's through doing a version of the film for Singapore or coming up with some material for their exhibitions, that's something that we've got to work out next year, but we would like to be able to share the story of Operation Jaywick both here and in Singapore.'

Sumption conceded that there has been an issue with the *Krait* being noticed in the past as people wandered past the floating collection and saw her as just another boat behind a locked gate. 'One of the benefits of taking it onto dry land is you can actually make it stable, and because it's wooden we can set up a display. What I wouldn't want to do is make it sacrosanct, so that you can't actually step on board, or go around. We would have the opportunity, I'm sure, to allow some access to the vessel both on board and below deck.

'To have [*Krait*] stable in an environmentally controlled place, I'm much more confident, fast-forward 200, 300 years, that that story will still be able to be told with that boat as it is now. Because that's our job. That's the real benefit of getting it out of the water.'

There is plenty of available science to support the successful displaying of timber vessels out of the water, with the *Vasa* Museum in Stockholm, Sweden, and the *Mary Rose* Museum in Portsmouth, England, two of the most famous, along with early Viking ships in Denmark.

'Visitors will be able to walk right up to the hull instead of viewing from a distance,' an ANMM flyer says. 'Instead of quietly floating at her berth, the new exhibit will bring the remarkable *Krait* and special forces story to life in a compelling way.'

19

Special capability lost

Using a navy submarine or an air force C-17 transport plane to deploy modern-day special forces troops is a highly complex process that requires a great deal of planning and coordination.

The chain of command is also complex: the army's Special Operations Command – the overall headquarters for SAS, Commandos and other special forces units – is under the operational commanders at Joint Operations Command (JOC) located near Canberra. Their ability to deploy over long distances depends on the RAAF for strategic airlift and the RAN for sealift.

For tactical (short range) airlift, the Sydney-based 2nd Commando Regiment, which includes the rapid response counter-terrorism Tactical Assault Group (TAG East) based at Holsworthy barracks, has its own specialised flight of Black Hawk helicopters so that it can deploy at a moment's notice.

Rick Moor and other ex–special forces operatives understand the strain on the military's finite resources, but they also appreciate the incredible benefits in special operations terms of units having their own strategic lift and support capabilities and not having to compete for transport space. Such a capability existed in mid-1945 but was gone just a few months later.

According to Moor attempts were made to rebuild the capability during the 1950s and '60s but the Vietnam War intervened and the focus on support factors was lost.

'Look at something like 200 Flight in 1945 – they did the longest operation on missions of any air force in the Second World War. They were picking people up from Leyburn [near Brisbane], flying them to Darwin then onto Morotai, then onto Southern Philippines and then into Borneo as one mission. So two overnight stops and three refuels but as one mission.'

More than 2000 Australian and foreign personnel served with SOA during World War II. It had a fleet of more than 20 high-speed and long-distance vessels based in Darwin, a flight of six Liberator aircraft, a range of highly specialised weapons and survival systems and very close ties with both the American and British Pacific submarine fleets.

Yet Moor said that capability was quickly lost because many of SOA's activities were so secret that only a small number of people actually knew about them, much less their scale and objectives.

'The Special Operations capability that they had in 1945 was more advanced than what we've got today in terms of breadth and scope,' Moor said. 'They'd integrated the full spectrum of subversive operations and intelligence gathering operations with their harassing operations or advanced raiding operations, with their guerrilla warfare capability and with their reconnaissance surveillance activity.

'Then between "M" Special Unit [coast watchers] and "Z" Special Unit, they had means of manning the organisation and they were able to draw on any stores they required so they had incredible flexibility.'

In addition to its organic capability, SOA also had well-established links with US aviation squadrons and USN fast boat and submarine fleets, as well as an extensive network of Australian-trained civilian operatives posted across the region.

This is why Rick Moor regards the *Krait* as a tangible symbol of a much bigger picture.

'It's an important national symbol because it introduces people to an incredible story,' he said. 'Whether people understand the complexity of the full story or not, that's not how that part of mythology serves. That mythology is part of the glue that holds civil society together. It's part of what you use to encourage and inspire individuals in your society and individuals in your military to strive for higher things. So, as a symbol I think it's incredibly important.

'Part of the reason that "Z" Special Unit was raised was not only to administer the army element of Special Operations Australia but also to manage the civilian operatives who were deployed and some of those were neutrals. The Portuguese were neutrals, the Timorese were neutrals, but they had to have a machine to pay and recognise them. So it was a very advanced capability.'

They also raised a large Indigenous force in Borneo and others in New Guinea, New Britain and Bougainville. The New Guinea force included an entire "M" Special battalion, established to administer the coast watchers and the local troops and police working for SOA. They had begun as a surveillance element but as the war progressed they developed into a fighting force.

Unfortunately, just months after the war had ended, the advanced special operations capability had disappeared from the Australian order of battle. Even the War Graves Unit, which was responsible for trying to identify the remains of Australians throughout the Pacific area of operations, was told by the army that there had been no Australians operating in areas where Caucasian bodies were being found. Many of them, as it turned out, were 'Z' Special Unit or 'M' Special Unit operatives whose presence was not known to the wider army, but only to a few senior officers.

Moor said the story of SOA is also the story of the integration of people from diverse ethnic backgrounds into Australian society when the White Australia policy was in full swing and well before the post-war migration boom.

'Special Operations Australia, unlike all other elements of Australian society at that stage, actively recruited other than white Australians,' he noted. 'It recruited Chinese, Malay, part-Japanese, part-Vietnamese Australians into the organisation and used them in an operational role and some such as Fred Sanderson and Jack Sue were incredibly brave and highly decorated and they did really quite remarkable things.'

Fred Sanderson was born in Bangkok and was a fluent Malay speaker when he parachuted into Borneo in March 1945 as part of Operation Semut (Malay for 'ant') 1. He had served in the Middle East at Tobruk and died in 1997 aged 87.

Perth-born Chinese Australian Jack Wong Sue was serving as a leading aircraftsman with the RAAF when he was recruited by 'Z' Special Unit to operate behind enemy lines in Borneo for an operation codenamed Agas 3. Sue was awarded the Distinguished Conduct Medal as a 19-year-old and would go on to be awarded the Medal of the Order of Australia before he died in Perth in 2009.

Another foreign-born operative, Abu Kassem, was marginalised in the general community back in Australia despite being awarded the Military Medal (MM) for his courage in the face of the enemy.

'They were about results. They were about what you were, not where you came from,' said Moor.

In a long overdue move, the AWM established a special forces exhibition in Canberra in 2017, with Operation Jaywick at its core and exploring the almost 20 years of continuous special forces involvement in recent conflicts in East Timor, Iraq and Afghanistan. Before that, special operations units had received only minimal recognition at the national shrine. The exhibition includes 660 objects, some on loan from individuals and families.

The AWM's assistant director Brian Dawson spent about six years in the SAS early in his army career. He admitted to having had only a limited knowledge of Jaywick and the wartime activities of 'Z' Special Unit during his time at the regiment.

'We hadn't rediscovered the history and of course a lot of the stuff was still highly classified – I mean, what happened in Borneo in 1945 wasn't declassified for decades afterwards,' he says.

These days Dawson is well and truly across the history and he regards Jaywick as a work of genius. 'The audacity of it is breathtaking and even now, when you read the story of Ivan Lyon and to some extent, [Bill] Reynolds coming up with this plan, working their way through the military bureaucracy, starting off in India then moving the base to Australia and then working their way up north, it's just an outrageously daring plan and the fact that they were able to pull it off is remarkable.'

Dawson draws comparisons between Operation Jaywick and the famous US Air Force 'Doolittle Raid' that took place in April 1942 when US Air Force Colonel Jimmy Doolittle led 16 B-25

Mitchell bombers from the aircraft carrier USS *Hornet* in an attack against Tokyo. Seventy of the 80 men who participated in the mission survived after crash-landing their unescorted and fuel-starved aircraft in China and Russia. That raid has become part of American military folklore.

The strategic impact of both missions was 'relatively minor', Dawson said, but they were both bold 'acts of defiance' that took the fight deep into enemy territory. 'The Doolittle Raid basically punched the Japanese Imperial Army and Navy on the nose in their backyard … If [Jaywick] had been publicised it would probably be in the same sort of category as [the way] the Doolittle Raid is viewed in the American history of the Second World War.'

Dawson acknowledged there is always a tension between special forces and the wider military hierarchy about the level of resources that should be devoted to what are often expensive and highly risky missions. 'Even the relatively improvised nature of the *Krait* raid still required an awful lot of organisation and logistics support to deliver those men well beyond enemy lines at a time when Australia was basically fighting for its life in 1942 and 1943.'

He says one of the great advantages of Ivan Lyon's plan was that it probably would never have passed any kind of 'staff college' test of proper procedure. 'The terrifying thought of a captain speaking directly to Wavell, who was probably a full general at that stage, and pushing these outrageous ideas was probably driving the military bureaucracy mad.'

Dawson also believes that the tension between Australia's wartime relationship with Britain and the United States probably played a part in why Operation Jaywick was not as lauded as it could have been at the time.

'Australia was caught between their instincts to go with the British model of special operations teams and the fact that we had handed over a significant amount of our sovereignty and military command to the Americans. In my view the interests of the British in postwar Southeast Asia and the interests of the Americans in postwar Southeast Asia were quite different,' he said.

Lyon's determination coupled with Donald Davidson's unwavering commitment to training as well as the lack of institutional hurdles, such as a proper risk assessment or frustrating modern-day occupational health and safety concerns, meant that the operation could be planned and conducted exactly as the two top men saw fit.

'For the young troops who volunteered to join them it was the ultimate adventure,' Dawson said. 'They were looking for adventure and you can imagine in one sense the freedom of going to a training base like Cairns or Fraser Island where you didn't have to worry about shaving and there wasn't an RSM [Regimental Sergeant Major] making your life a misery, but it was full-on hard soldiering: learning all about new weapons, demolitions, learning communications and medical stuff, which would have been "wow!" for the young soldiers. It was a brand new and exciting world – and then you are told you can't talk to anybody about it. The same psychology still applies today.'

Another element to the strategy of employing special forces in highly complex operations such as Rimau and Jaywick was the lack of control and integration of the so-called 'pin prick' operations in the overall war plan.

'We know with the benefit of hindsight that the submarine war against the Japanese merchant navy was much more effective in a strategic sense,' he said. 'You can only really say that after the war. At the time, I think they were looking for anything that sounded like it might produce a success. Given the resources that needed to be attracted to these special forces operations, they needed to be seen to be doing something and not just sitting there training endlessly on Fraser Island. You had to actually get into the fight at some stage.'

Such shortcomings were less evident in later and better-planned 'Z' Special Unit operations such as Semut and Agas in Borneo, where the operatives had their own aircraft to call on for insertion. However, they still relied on the courage and cunning of well-trained individuals for their success.

'In the high-level, clear and rapid communications world that we live in now it's hard to cast your mind back to where these guys jumped out and they're not heard from for a week or so,' Dawson said.

In some places, such as East Timor, where the enemy had broken the Allied codes, some operatives jumped from a Liberator and were never heard from again.

Jim Truscott is firmly in the camp that says Lyon should have received a posthumous VC.

'Ivan Lyon was a driving force behind both of them, no doubt and that itself is just a feat of human endeavour,' he said. 'Lyon should have been given a Victoria Cross. That's long overdue, long overdue. Problem is, he's British, you see. He's not an Australian. You can't give a Pom an Australian Victoria Cross and why would anyone in the British special forces community now — they did so much in Europe — be worried about this nutter that they sent out to Australia?'

SAVING THE
KRAIT

20

The detective story

The daunting job of figuring out exactly what the *Krait* had looked like during Operation Jaywick fell to the ANMM's curator of historic vessels David Payne, assisted by the man who knew the boat better than most – naval surveyor Warwick Thomson.

Before tenders could be invited or any work carried out in 2017–18, it was up to these two men to conduct the extensive research required to decide exactly where every hatch and bulkhead had been located on the *Krait* in 1943.

Previous restoration work on the vessel, particularly the extensive 1982 Ballina refit – which had been specified in detail by the AWM in the loan agreement with the maritime museum – had the major advantage of the living memories of several Jaywick survivors.

These included radio operator Horrie Young, who not only had a clear memory of the configuration and had advised an earlier refit at Palm Beach in 1977, but also technical drawings of the vessel; and Moss Berryman, the former able seaman and reserve canoeist for the mission.

Both operatives had spent the additional fortnight living on the boat while the attack on Singapore harbour took place and during its aftermath, as the *Krait* hid among the inlets and islands of southern Borneo waiting to retrieve the six raiders and their folding canoes.

By 2017 Berryman was the only survivor. Like Horrie Young, he had maintained a close postwar interest in the *Krait*. As well as being on board when she returned to Sydney Harbour in 1964, he and his family were treated to a private cruise several years ago. They had visited the ANMM where Berryman introduced himself and was ushered in to meet the director Kevin Sumption and other officials.

'We went down the walkway to where it was stationed,' Moss recalled, 'and there were a couple of chaps working on it. So [our escort] said to them, "Start up the engine, this is Moss Berryman, he wants to steer it around the harbour." So, they started it up and we backed out and I drove it around part of the lower end of Sydney Harbour and back we went and gave the family a thrill. We weren't tearing along – we were only doing about four or five knots – but they got the feel of the thing. And the old Gardner diesel that we put in it in the middle of 1943 is still going like a charm.'

Berryman is happy that the *Krait* is being restored and properly looked after although he remains firmly in the 'leave it in the water' camp. He questioned the need to spend millions on an internal display when hospitals and schools are badly short of funds and said he would be happy to see her remain in the water for the next 50 years or more.

While her long-term future is being debated, the objective of the new refurbishment was to stabilise any deterioration and to restore her as closely as possible to the 1943 configuration. With Berryman the only surviving witness and some of the information provided in earlier surveys incorrect, it proved to be a challenging task.

Payne and Thomson spent hours poring over drawings and images as they investigated every square millimetre of the vessel, confirming and speculating about where a particular tank, hatch, locker or bulkhead had been located.

David Payne is not the sort of bloke to be put off by a lack of evidence or by a major challenge. A studious but highly enthusiastic character, his respect for the *Krait* and the men who sailed in her runs deep and his love of the task is infectious.

Payne grew up in Mosman on Sydney Harbour and his uncle, the well-known naval architect Alan Payne, decided to employ the self-taught young yacht designer after he created some impressive 12-foot (3.6-metre) skiffs. He later designed an 18-footer (5.5-metre) as well.

'My uncle was winding down his business and he needed a draftsman,' Payne said.

Alan Payne's most famous works were the two America's Cup challengers, *Gretel* and *Gretel 2*, which he designed and built for Sir Frank Packer. Another of his timber racing yachts, *Nocturne*, took line honours in the 1952 Sydney to Hobart Yacht Race. The Payne family's links with boats stretch back to their English ancestors, who were watermen on the Thames River during the 1850s. Young David's father had also had yachts and he had sailed 12-foot skiffs from an early age. David jumped at the chance to learn from his uncle, the master.

Both David and Alan worked as consultants to the maritime museum. After his uncle died in 1995, David kept up the museum work and has been the curator of historic vessels since 2004. Part of his early consultancy work at the museum included drawing up plans for historic vessels where no plans had previously existed. Those plans were then used by the museum to restore a vessel to its original configuration.

When the AWM and the ANMM decided to restore the *Krait* to her 1943 configuration as phase one of their eventual permanent display, David Payne was the obvious candidate to conduct the work, along with Thomson and museum fleet manager and former navy officer Damien Allan.

When Payne joined the museum staff he became manager of the Australian Register of Historic Vessels where the details of some 600 vessels that are not displayed at the museum are recorded.

'Once I began doing that research work it wasn't long before they started to get me to draw a few things again and we've done a few other restorations on a couple of boats where I've done the plans, which ultimately led to this one with the *Krait*,' he said.

Fortunately, the fleet surveyor and timber boat enthusiast Warwick Thomson volunteered to assist. The first thing that they had to do was gather all the information that existed about the vessel including plans that were held by the AWM. As soon as they received the plans they took them on board the *Krait*, where they found some obvious errors.

'People had miscounted frames, which is significant because you've got to lay out the frames as to where things are going to be. They had made mistakes with the dimensions of some of the things that were on there and made the boat longer or shorter or whatever. There were errors,' Payne said.

The next step was to cross-reference the plans with photographs from the time. Fortunately, the war memorial had some 14 or so high-resolution images of the *Krait* in her wartime guise and the two men sat down with a magnifying glass to compare the reality with the plans. They also read all the available material about Operation Jaywick and the vessel and found a number of contradictions concerning the boat.

'I actually went through them, literally writing in a notebook any dimension, anything they'd put down and then cross-referenced it all. So, we had three sources of information. What's written in the books, what's in the photographs and what's on the plans,' Payne says.

'Some of the information proved to be quite misleading because when you looked at the fine print you realised this was actually drawn by someone who was on the boat in 1944 and 1945. He's probably picked up on things that have been added to the boat and not necessarily exactly where I'd already seen some of the things written. I then went back to the drawing board and drew it out, until eventually I felt this was where they probably had to be.

'It takes a few goes backwards and forwards and a hell of a lot of rubbing out before finally realising, yeah, this is all gelling, all that is pretty reasonable; I might be this far out, I might be a little bit closer but it's got to be as close as you're going to get given that you can't ask someone exactly where something was.'

Using that information, he formulated an accurate outline of the boat assisted by a listed lines plan that was drawn accurately by an architectural draftsman at Garden Island dockyard.

'The only problem was that the prints were a bit warped but I knew what the scale was so I could draw it out again on the big scale,' he says. 'I've got a block that I could fit everything else into and then correlate exactly where certain frames fell relative to certain parts, elaborate the rest of the boat and get the skeleton drawn up.'

They were then able to add the bits and pieces required from the 1943 fit-out, as well as determining where hatches were located and their exact size. 'A key starting point in this whole process of piecing the boat back together from 1943 was the fact that the four compartments were divided up with bulkheads and we needed to establish where those bulkheads were.'

Payne's beautiful colour drawing of the 1943 *Krait* appears in the picture section of this book.

Payne and Thomson spent many hours on board the boat and applied their experience and logic to determine where the bulkheads had been fitted for the Jaywick raid. At last they were confident that they had the spots within a frame or two. They then cross-referenced their observations with details from several books and the recollections of Young and Berryman.

Young had died in 2011 so the final step was for Payne to take his plans to Adelaide for a face-to-face chat with Berryman. Once Moss had explained in great detail how the whole show had almost come to a bitter end when the Japanese warship challenged them in the Lombok Strait, David Payne was able to steer him back to his drawings.

'I learn a lot more, because I didn't really know what to ask about. He just spontaneously said, "Oh, we did this, we did that" and that would prompt another thing in other areas, and I'd ask him, "Well, what do you think about what I've drawn there?" And he would say, "Yes, I think that's about right," or "It could have been like this." Or, for example, the fuel tanks, which are still an issue that — I'm not sure, I know I've resolved and I think Warwick is very happy with it, but we'll bring it up one more time before we do something about it.'

Berryman did not know much about the fuel tanks, having had very little to do with that aspect of the mission. His job had been to maintain the high readiness of the weapons and to keep his fitness up in case he had to join a canoe.

'He said, "No, I don't know anything about the fuel tanks because I never went down there. All I can tell you is we topped up tanks that were below deck from some drums that were on top at some point." I said, "Okay, well that kind of makes sense,"' says Payne. 'There was something down there, we've just got to resolve in our minds whether the drawings of those tanks that have come up in these 1944–45 things are actually drawings of tanks that were there. We tend to think so, because there's a lot of tank volume there and we do know it's been said by a couple of people they had a get-out source in that, in terms of range. On the way back, if the strait was closed they could go to Hawaii or they could go to South Africa, so that's a lot of fuel.'

Payne said it was crucial that the restoration work be as accurate as possible given the lack of original drawings and surviving eyewitnesses. The large-scale exterior items were easiest due to photographs of the vessel in Jaywick mode, but establishing the exact location for internal structures such as bulkheads and lockers was much more challenging.

There was a certain logic to the process, but with such a specialised mission there were unique elements throughout the vessel that had to be fitted into the restoration sequence. These included storage lockers for the Bren and Owen machine guns that had to be available at short notice and then deployed through firing hatches cut into the timber awning fitted above the stern.

This is where the personal recollections of Moss Berryman and the diary entries of Horrie Young were so helpful to Payne and Warwick Thomson.

'The hatches had to fit a stripped-down Bren or Owen gun and they had to be assembled and ready to engage in about 20 seconds. So I would draw it and they would say if it could work or not,' Payne said. 'It's stuff like that that they are really helpful with, and it has allowed us to get this, I'm sure, a lot closer to being right than we would have been able to do otherwise.'

The process of developing accurate drawings based on human accounts and old photos is like a detective story, Payne said. 'That's why you draw in pencil so you can rub the damn thing out and not draw everything out.'

When he first drew the awning, for example, he knew it was wrong, but couldn't put his finger on the exact reason. Once he had worked out the correct angles and the location of the hatches relative to the internal fit-out he was able to get the detail right. 'We set up the hatches and then worked out that I actually had them drawn a bit too far aft because that's where the water tank is going to be and they'll probably want to stand in the middle of that hatch to lean on it.'

So he moved the hatches forward and to the size that they appeared in the photographs before he showed the drawings to Moss Berryman, who remembered that they had opened in a particular direction. 'He knew [that], because he had to stand up in it and that was the reverse of what we thought – so it wasn't opening the right way.'

Berryman's insights were also invaluable when it came to the working area on the stern of the vessel where the crew spent most of their time. It was also where the galley (such as it was) was located as well as the ship's 'toilet' – which was simply two handholds attached to the gunwale over the stern.

'We had to sit on the back and we weren't allowed to use toilet paper or anything, I just remember two handholds,' Berryman told him.

Payne spent hours with him, poring over the drawings and photographs and discussing where various items were located throughout the vessel.

'Moss said he had slept amongst some 44-gallon drums and there were two hatches that they could use as well as an existing entry hatch. We had to make a call and felt, well, the hatch where it is at the moment is probably where it was,' Payne says. 'It makes a lot of sense and there's some sort of stowage and sleeping behind there, which makes sense too.'

For exhibition purposes, Payne and Thomson wanted the *Krait* to resemble her wartime guise on a given day.

'On one particular day in September [1943] they took the mast and the aerial and the whole rig down and laid it on the side of the deck so that they would lower the profile of the boat,' Payne said. 'We can make *Krait* look exactly like it did that day. We can actually say, "On this day, this is how this boat looked." And it will have the folboats stowed, it will have all that fit-out down the back, it will have sacks of potatoes; things that they apparently had there. It will have the sleeping gear that they slept on, on top of the deck, the 44-gallon drums that were tied on.'

It will also include the dinghy that was modified to attack enemy ships. The replica three-metre (10-foot) clinker boat will be fitted with the breathing pipes and leather hand straps that Davidson had planned to use to attach mines to any enemy ship that intercepted the vessel – an idea that Payne regards as 'lunacy'.

'We can get all of that right because Moss has remembered so many things. We want to make it look like that 1943 [day]. It's just such a rare opportunity to do it. I've never really been able to peel a boat down that accurately.'

As for the courage and audacity of the entire crew, Payne said, 'I don't think they perhaps ever really thought about how marginal it was at some time. But it was a very different time, and they had confidence. They did have people that were seamen on there that understood things. They had an engineer who understood his engine because he'd finally got one that he liked – the Gardner – and they really had a good engine then.'

Payne's father flew bombers during World War II and while he did not discuss his war much with his son, he did open up to his grandsons when they asked him about the sense of danger. 'He said, "We got around that because we were trained – we actually had good training – and we just stuck to our job. I had to fly the plane, so that's what I did. I was the pilot; I just concentrated on that. I left it to the others to do their job, and that's how you got around the element of fear and so on. You did it and you came back and you did it three nights later or 10 days later."'

Payne said Operation Jaywick was even more risky – and the men were thrown into it, because most of them did not even know the objective until after they left Exmouth.

'It's hard for us to put ourselves in those situations and understand [but] they were there as a group supporting each other,' he said. 'Strong leadership gets you round all that, so you just get on with the job. You've got a job to do; do it, it will work.'

Payne is also in awe of Bill Reynolds, the man who was the *Krait*'s master during the evacuation of Singapore and, with Lyon, was the brains behind the Jaywick raid. It was Reynolds who had realised that the enemy would not fire upon a Japanese fishing boat as he carried hundreds of refugees away from Singapore in the dark days of early 1942.

'Reynolds decided that the best way [was] not to cut and run as though you were escaping, but rather go back out the way a fishing boat would go back to Singapore, go up through the strait and out the top end,' Payne said. 'No one's going to shoot at me then because I'm going in the wrong direction. I thought that was brilliant and this seems to be about the only boat around that relates back to that episode. So I related that back to Dunkirk, and how they valued those boats enormously in England.

'It's also so important for the commandos, because what else have they got to hang onto in terms of artefacts from that era? So much of it has been lost. There might be a few little examples of weapons and things but they were probably never actually used, because that's the only way they survived. They were spares or whatever. This boat got used. You can stand on the deck and say, "My God, this thing was there at the time." It is enormously significant that the *Krait* managed to survive, it's there, it's still in a sense operational and it can tell its story. We've just got to get it looking the way it can, to interpret that story. We know that story is significant and we know we can do it accurately.'

Men such as Payne and Thomson, who have spent their lives messing about with boats, seem to possess a kind of sixth sense when it comes to interpreting the story of an old vessel.

Warwick Thomson served his apprenticeship at the Union Steam Ship Company at its headquarters in Day Street, Sydney close to Darling Harbour. The firm had workshops on the third floor of its inner-city building, but most of the work performed by shipwrights was conducted on ships docked somewhere in the harbour. His father's uncle was a World War I veteran and prominent Sydney businessman Sil Rohu, who invented the famous Vaucluse Junior (VJ) sailing dinghy designed and built at the Vaucluse Sailing Club in the early 1930s.

213

Many famous yachtsmen and women began their sailing careers in the VJ. It was designed in such a way that it could be built at home and that children and teenagers could learn to sail in a safe and stable craft. It was designed for a crew of two, virtually unsinkable and easy to right if it capsized. The idea was that the young sailors would then graduate at age 18 to open skiff classes.

'My cousins used to sail VJs and I sort of was interested in sailing from that time,' Thomson said. He raced 12-foot skiffs with the Lane Cove club for some 50 years.

After gaining his shipwright ticket he transferred to Garden Island to work and obtained his naval architecture certificate. Thirty years later he was still at the island dockyard. He had married his wife, Jen, in 1970 and they raised two daughters at their home of 45 years in Gladesville above Looking Glass Bay, just across from Banjo Paterson's former residence, with sweeping views over the Parramatta River to Abbotsford 12ft Sailing Club.

Thomson became a naval surveyor and spent many years working for Defence and surveying navy ships around Australia. After retiring, he worked as a contractor to the navy, before receiving a phone call from the maritime museum's deputy director Peter Rout, who had known him in their Cockatoo Island days.

'Peter said, "We haven't had a survey done on *Vampire* for 20-odd years and yours is the last name on the survey report." So that's how I started at the maritime museum,' Thomson said. That was 2006 and he stayed on staff until 2012, when he again retired to become a contractor for the second time. His hobby was restoring timber boats and he inherited Sil Rohu's 28-foot (8.5-metre) ranger class boat, *Maluka*, which went on to win its class in the Sydney to Hobart Yacht Race.

Thomson regarded it as an honour to be involved with the *Krait* project. Although he had worked on the boat as part of his job at the museum and was very familiar with the story of Operation Jaywick, it was not until he met Douglas Herps that he really understood the significance of the vessel to the veteran and special forces communities, especially the former members of 'Z' Special Unit.

When Herps told him that he wanted to take it out of the water Thomson was slightly taken aback because as a shipwright he would always prefer to keep a timber boat in the water.

'After a time, I could see his point of view,' he said, 'and the reports from the Australian War Memorial on the conservation do in fact admit that in the long term that is the best solution — to have it out of the water and properly preserved and stored. I've been over to the Western Australian Maritime Museum and they've done it very well over there. So I've got no doubt that, yes, it can be done — but it takes certainly a lot of effort and a lot of finance to actually get it to that stage.'

Thomson often went over to the Herps home in Woollahra and the men would talk over a cup of tea about what needed to be done to preserve the *Krait*. This included the funding and how Douglas was planning to approach the stakeholders.

'We developed a very strong friendship and Douglas probably influenced me more than anything else about the importance of the 'Z' Special Unit and the sort of men who served in it.'

Thomson regarded the *Krait* as being just as important to the maritime museum as its major warships, the destroyer HMAS *Vampire* and submarine HMAS *Onslow* but believed it had even greater significance because of the success of the Jaywick raid.

'It is absolutely necessary that we keep that history alive in the vessel itself and I think the way we are doing it, if it comes to fruition, I think we will achieve it,' he said. 'After all, "Z" Special was the start of the SAS and I think Douglas always had it in mind that there would be a progression of displays from "Z" up to the present day.'

He said the homage paid to the *Krait* extends beyond the veterans, historians, shipwrights and museum volunteers to the general public and overseas visitors as well.

'I've been doing some work on *Krait* and people come up (and these are people not just from Australia but from Britain and other places) to say, "Oh yeah I recognise *Krait* for her exploits during the war." I had one young bloke come up whose father had served on *Krait* up in Darwin in 1945. He just came out of the blue. There's a lot of interest from the public, not just from people who are involved in maritime history.'

21

The shipwrights

When the refit and restoration specifications went out to tender in 2016, the first task on the scope of works was to strip all the paint off the *Krait*'s hull so the shipwrights could get a decent idea of what the planking was actually like.

'Unfortunately, the topside planking was in relatively poor condition,' Warwick Thomson said. 'And one of the reasons for that was that in the past it had been painted with a water-based paint, which actually draws the moisture into the timber. I believe that was part of the reason at least that that topside timber deteriorated.'

A survey conducted during the 1982 refit in Ballina had estimated that just 20 per cent of the original teak remained in the vessel. When Thomson surveyed her on the slips he found that about 67 per cent was in fact teak or Australian hardwood. That meant that most of the timber below the waterline was in a much better shape than he expected. The big surprise was above the waterline; between the bulwark and the waterline, where most of the timber was rotten and had to be replaced. Another bonus was the fact that the *Krait*'s keel had not sagged or 'hogged' where it bends towards the bow and stern, creating a 'hog's back' effect.

Given the importance of the vessel it was with great relief that Thomson was able to recommend master shipwright Michael Bartley at Woolwich on Sydney Harbour as the successful tenderer.

During the final years and months of his life, Douglas Herps spent a great deal of time at the maritime museum talking to the shipwrights and volunteers and anyone else with an interest in the *Krait*.

'Douglas used to come alongside when there was a chap who was looking after it, Jimmy Christodoulou, one of our shipwrights at the maritime museum. I met Douglas through Jim,' Warwick Thomson said. 'Jim was in charge of maintenance on the *Krait* and he took a keen interest in the history as well.'

Jim Christodoulou spent 12 years working at the maritime museum and most of that time was spent on the *Krait*. Born in Greece, he came to Australia with his parents as a seven-year-old and began his shipwright apprenticeship at a small yard on Longnose Point in Birchgrove. When it closed he moved to the Union Steam Ship Company where he completed his time in 1973 before working as a relief shipwright mainly around the Balmain area.

He then went to sea with several different steam-ship companies including BHP and Australian National Lines (ANL) until 1980, when he returned to shore with Howard Smith's boatyard at Birchgrove. He joined Sydney Ferries at their maintenance yard in Balmain before leaving the trade for several years to work at North Ryde RSL. He started at the ANMM in 2005, retiring in January 2018.

Christodoulou regards the *Krait* as a 'relatively young' boat in terms of historic timber vessels. While teak vessels were built to last, they were fixed with galvanised fastenings that 'blew out' well before the timber deteriorated.

'As a work boat, she was probably made to last 30 years and that was when the fastenings would go, but as far as timber goes she is not that old. We have boats at the museum that are 130 years old,' he said.

During his time at the museum he did a lot of reading about the *Krait* and Operation Jaywick. He used to read on his meal breaks, perched in the boat's wheelhouse where much of the action of Operation Jaywick was centred.

Phase One of the boat's restoration finally received the green light in late 2016 after a two-year battle to raise the necessary funds and she was slipped at Bartley's yard in Woolwich on a two-metre tide in December 2016.

Unfortunately, despite Douglas Herps's passionate lobbying, the corporate sector had shown little interest and the bulk of the money for the initial restoration phase came from the ANMM and the AWM, the Australian Army and some smaller, private donations, including $50,000 from the Herps Family Trust.

The $1.1 million project was enough to refurbish the structure of the vessel, the planking and decking, to prevent freshwater ingress and rotting and to ensure she remained seaworthy for many years to come.

After winning the tender, one of Michael Bartley's first tasks was physically getting the vessel onto his slipway and up into his boatshed.

The shed had to be modified to allow the boat to fit in without blocking the rest of the facility so the team could continue working on other vessels.

Bartley was confident that his staff, including his apprentices, had the skill sets to complete the job, even though very few of them had ever touched a heavy-plank boat before. He was very familiar with heavy-plank vessels, having served his apprenticeship at the Cockatoo Island dockyard just across the water from his slipway.

'We had a series of 40-foot [12-metre] timber workboats which serviced the island and they were also the boats that pushed the barges around,' he said. 'We worked on a lot of what they call "black yachts", which are big timber barges which don't really exist anymore. Most of them have been cut up by now but they might be 50 or 60 feet [15 or 18 metres long and 30 feet [nine metres] wide, and they would carry all the timber, the metal, everything on and off the island. They were sort of work barges. So we were continually repairing them. They'd get full of worm and you'd have to chop planks out.'

Unlike the teak used in the *Krait*, the work barges were built from the cheaper and less durable Oregon timber. Most of his experience with teak had been in decking rather than planking timbers, so he was also on a learning curve with *Krait*. 'There were a few navy boats that we worked on, officers' launches built in the 1950s, which were solid teak. Teak is the premium timber to use but it's expensive and now it's very hard to get, and to get the quality for boat planking is difficult.'

He was only able to source enough teak locally for part of the hull and deck repairs; the rest had to be obtained from overseas with the proper import controls.

'Things are changing, it's getting harder and harder to get that timber out now. A lot of the forests have been completely closed. So that's been the biggest challenge – just acquiring the timber for the job.'

Fortunately, despite massive deforestation, the forests of Myanmar (Burma) are still yielding some quality product and he was able to obtain enough for the *Krait* restoration project.

The biggest challenge was the scale of the available boards. 'It's difficult to get the quality quarter-sawn deck boards that we need and instead of being able to get six- and eight-metre lengths, about 4.2 metres [was] the longest we were able to get for the job,' he said.

That meant more butts and joins in the structure and because they could not obtain the original seven-centimetre-thick boards they had to settle for five-centimetre thickness, which meant laminating another board to the top.

'With modern glues and quality fastenings we're not compromising the strength at all. It's more a matter of just the fact of time and the scarcity of the quality lengths and widths of teak boards now.'

Replacing teak planks is not an easy job. 'The planks have all got shape cut to them, there is twist and bend in them to give the shape of the boat,' he explained.

A plank that might start at 300 millimetres wide could end up at 200 millimetres wide due to the curve of the vessel. Such is the amount of guesswork when estimating requirements for old timber boats while they are in the water that the amount of planking required for the *Krait* more than doubled from the initial estimate. But one thing was certain: the vessel was sturdy and well constructed.

'The older boats were always heavily timbered,' Bartley said. 'They didn't have a lot of machinery to mill timber down. It was easy to build them bigger and give you the extra strength that you need to make them last, and that's because it's a framed boat and the planks are planked on frame. The frames have really stood the test of time.'

When he tendered for the job Bartley assumed he would have to bring in some experienced older shipwrights to assist with the refurbishment. However, his young shipwrights, labourers and apprentices all stepped up to the plate, and in the process, became very aware of the significance of the *Krait* and her story.

'It is a credit to them,' he said. 'I felt it would be a bit of a slap in the face to them if I brought in other guys to work on the job. They're here day in day out and take the good with the bad, because we don't always have glamorous work. Sometimes it's pretty ordinary and pretty ugly.'

Bartley's wife and business partner, Catriona, said that many of the old skills, such as steaming timber planks, that are required when working on a vessel such as the *Krait* are barely used anymore. Steaming involves super heating timber in a steam vessel and shaping the planks to bend to the shape of the vessel.

'Some of the planks had a lot of shape in them,' Bartley explained. 'And we couldn't set them cold, so we had a stainless steel keg (a beer keg) filled with water and a big burner underneath it to boil the water. The resulting steam goes into a simple plywood box with a flange in the bottom of it. We'd fill that box up with steam, whack the planks in, pack it full of rags and caulk [to seal] the planks. It's roughly an inch an hour is how long you're meant to steam a plank.'

No plank of timber fitted in a wooden boat is ever dead straight and some even have an S-shape. When dealing with 50-millimetre thick and very hard teak planks bending and shaping them without cutting becomes a major challenge.

'The steaming process softens it enough that you can jam one end in, fasten it off and then with Acrows [metal props] and lumps of timber and Spanish windlasses and ratchet straps and whatever else, big clamps and wind it in and you leave it clamped up usually overnight. The clamp cools down and it sets in shape then.'

These are ancient skills in the shipwright trade but they are skills that young men more used to using an app on their mobile phones are keen to learn. Bartley was happy to pass them on because he had been fortunate enough to learn them as part of his early training.

'We built a thing called a jolly boat over at Cockatoo Island,' he recalled. 'It was for a re-enactment of the [first settler] landing in the Lane Cove River. The money was put up by sponsor and we built that boat out of a Filipino cedar called calantas and tea tree and the tea tree was grown in frames,' he says. 'We weren't allowed to use any power tools. We had to cut it all by hand, take all the faces of the tea tree off and cut the garboard seam [the plates next to the keel] and shape the keel blocks with an axe and hand planes and spokeshaves [tool used to smooth down timber]. And then that was screw-fastened, which again is a different way to seal the edges of the planks together.'

He said the planks for that boat were actually boiled rather than steamed.

'Old George, our superintendent, was a real hard head and he had this theory that it was better to boil the planks than to steam them. They get just as wet when you steam them and steam is a lot hotter than boiling water so I tend to agree to disagree with him on that one. We actually had to make a fire, a wood fire and we had a big steel pipe and we'd fill the pipe with water and build a fire under the end of this big pipe and then stuff the planks in.'

When they removed the deck timbers that had been fitted to the *Krait* in Ballina they found that all the deck beams were in the wrong position, according to David Payne's drawings. They also discovered that the hatches were about 200 millimetres too small.

'It was a matter of moving all the beams, repositioning, lining them all up, lofting out the new deck for the new hatch layout and then cutting and fitting new deck carlins [structural timbers running fore and aft between the beams] to suit the hatch sizes,' Bartley said. 'And of course, that also meant new tie rods because the tie rods were in the wrong position to be adjacent to beams. So, it created a few more challenges and set us back a little bit in the timing.'

Bartley was pleasantly surprised by the lack of major shocks when it came to the structural integrity of the boat, due largely to the fact that her builders had been able to over-engineer her with fully grown timbers.

'The lighter-frame boats, the boats with lighter scantlings, tend not to stand the test of time, whereas she's so heavily built and the quality of timber that was used originally has kept her in good stead,' he said. 'You never know with boats what you're going to find until you start to get down to the bare bones. Decks come off and all sorts of things present themselves as being a bit of a challenge. It's all part and parcel with the sort of handcraft that we do.'

In Bartley's view, depending on the standard of maintenance there was no reason why the *Krait* could not last in the water for another 40 years or more.

'She is still majority iron-fastened, so fastenings do corrode and things do move but there's no reason why it couldn't last out the same lifetime it's already had. Given that the new deck will be caulked with Oakum and puttied up with Marine Pitch, that will stop the fresh water getting through and it's the fresh water that does the damage. [If] the guys at the museum manage to keep plenty of salt water into the boat inside and outside, there's no reason why we can't keep her going for a long time.'

The final challenge for Bartley and his team would be getting the vessel off the slipway and back into Sydney Harbour. With all her new timbers she weighed considerably more than when she was first slipped.

After 14 months on the slipway such a heavy vessel could be difficult to shift safely and with a large marina full of boats aft of the slipway the need for caution was paramount.

By the end of 2017, shipwright Andrew Stephenson estimated that about 90 per cent of the major structural issues with the hull planking and the underwater woodwork had already been completed at the boatyard.

'There were quite a few significant problems that have been waiting for a number of years now and it's really good to get them addressed,' he said. 'It is a fishing boat, so quality isn't of the essence, but it was quite heavily overbuilt for what it is. So, like quite large frames all really close together and that's sort of the thing that's kept it going for so long and will keep it going into the future.'

Provided the work was done correctly, then he regarded the idea of conserving the vessel out of the water was a good one.

'I don't know the science behind it, but as long as it's done in a good way, it would be a really good thing. Boats are built to be in the water but it would certainly be an awesome thing to look at out of the water. Actually, it certainly is an awesome thing to look at out of the water,' said the young man, who spent a year doing just that.

There is all-round agreement that the deep maintenance and restoration work undertaken by Michael Bartley and his team must be followed up with a comprehensive maintenance schedule and particularly with a weekly all-over soaking with salt water that had occurred during her time on the slipway.

Bartley points out that in the context of some historic timber vessels around the world, a well-built 1934 teak vessel is relatively young.

'I think, realistically, it needs a cover for the decks to keep some of the sun off, just because the UV does so much damage and the heat,' he said. 'Remember when these boats were built they were always wet. They always had salt water over the decks. They had pumps running, they were workboats, so they were always getting dunked and that stops the timber drying out. The reason this deck has fallen apart so badly is because it [has been allowed to] dry out so badly, and all the planks have shrunk and the seams, the caulking has fallen out and then fresh water has run in. Every time it rains it gets soaked.'

But for 23-year-old shipwright Brendan Jenkins, after more than a year working on the *Krait* which he regarded as a privilege after learning the story of a group of men about his age, there was no doubt that she should be in the water.

'It needs the salt water to keep it going, to stop any rot and keep the timber all swollen up,' he said. 'Until they come up with something, I mean I've seen in other museums, they're mainly replicas that are kept inside the museums. So they're built out of different timber but she's an old girl, so she has a fair bit of movement in her. And so I think until they come up with something that can probably keep it moist enough to have it displayed out of the water, I think it should just be in the water. They need to use it, bring it out on Anzac Day and stuff like that. Just to show the boat off. I think it's the best thing for a start so everyone knows about it. If boats don't get used then everything stops working.'

Seeing the structural restoration work underway was a source of great joy for Warwick Thomson. 'They are doing a fantastic job at Michael Bartley's, the young blokes that are working on it – and they are young blokes,' he said in late 2017. 'Michael's got some excellent workmen there, shipwrights and apprentices and they're all keen to do it and I think there's good work ethic going on. These blokes are used to working on highly polished expensive cruisers and yachts so this basic shipwright work is another dimension for them as well. I believe that all round we definitely picked the right contractor to do the work.'

Thomson said the *Krait*'s long-term welfare would depend entirely on the standard of work undertaken at Bartley's slipway.

'We've got to get the vessel's structural and watertight integrity right,' he said. 'Get that right and preserved in the way that we need to have it and it won't matter what plan is adopted for the long term, as far as taking it out of the water is concerned. My aim is to actually get that vessel itself in the condition that it's going to survive and unless we do that we're kidding ourselves. They are doing a good job and I'm quite sure that it's going to last for many, many years even in the water.'

Indeed, the boat could be in the water for many years to come if funding is not forthcoming for the out-of-water display. The money for the first phase of the restoration work by Bartley and his crew was hard-won and the vessel was to return to the maritime museum to have the final 1943 restoration work carried out.

'The configuration work can be done in water, fitting the bulkheads, fitting out the galley, all of that sort of stuff can be done in water,' Thomson said. 'It just would have been a lot easier had the deck been off and they'd been able to fit the bulkheads in with the workshop right next to them. But it can be done in the water, there's no doubt about that.'

The 2014 stakeholder survey turned up an overwhelming view that the *Krait* should be removed from the water and preserved for all time. In 2015 the ANMM and AWM signed an agreement, 'to develop a long-term plan for the conservation, interpretation and display of MV *Krait* in a shore-based facility at Darling Harbour'.

For museum curators and expert conservators the decision to remove the *Krait* from the water is a no-brainer, but for many shipwrights and old salts, any sound boat should always be kept in the water. David Payne said that, as one shipwright put it, 'you could love this thing [*Krait*] to death'.

'The worst thing you could do is pull it out and put it straight on display and find that three years later the whole thing is literally exploded in front of you and you've got a real problem,' he says. 'You've got to make sure you address those things early on and have the answers in place and move it the fewest number of times possible. We need to know when that end position is going to be, and see how many times we actually have to move it to get it to there.'

Even if the *Krait* were eventually displayed out of the water in a controlled environment she would still require a great deal of maintenance. 'It's a different sort of maintenance but it still requires regular checking and regular observation of what's going on and they still require items being taken off and replaced'.

With two tiers of government and an increasingly tight corporate sector yet to be convinced of its merits, no one believes that the indoor display area for the *Krait* will be built any time soon.

ANMM director Kevin Sumption regards the permanent out-of-water display of the *Krait* as vital to the vessel's long-term future but he is not expecting it to happen overnight. 'The longer it stays in the water, the less of the original fabric of not only the 1934 fishing vessel but the 1943 vessel is there, because the mere fact you're sitting in water means eventually timbers get saturated, timbers will be affected by the environment and they ultimately will need to be replaced,' he said. 'So, my hope is in the next five to ten years we can make the transition out of the water into a purpose-built facility that will also allow it to continue to operate as a memorial to commemorate service.'

The museum's 2016 vessel management plan for the *Krait* incorporates a detailed maintenance schedule that includes daily inspections, a weekly deck wash down with seawater and engine run and battery check, a monthly run for all systems and safety gear and a six-monthly paintwork inspection and repair.

The plan also specifies that every 12 months the vessel should be dry-docked and surveyed for pest infestation, and the hull surveyed, cleaned, repainted and audited. After five years the engine and machinery should be overhauled and the planking and structure assessed.

Following the 2017–18 refurbishment, the *Krait*'s operations will be strictly limited to reduce the risk of damage or loss. As much maintenance work as possible will be carried out at the wharf, which would also provide an opportunity to train junior shipwrights in wooden vessel construction techniques and the mechanical operation of the vessel.

Before he became ill with cancer, Warwick Thomson summed up perfectly just what the *Krait* project was all about: 'It's got to be that hands-on touchy-feely end product because it's an incredible history. It's something we should never lose sight of.'

Due to his serious illness he was unable to oversee the final stages of the refurbishment but had absolutely no qualms about the work that was being done. 'I'm just sorry I can't be there all the time to sort of support them,' he said while undergoing treatment.

Sadly, he died in March 2018 so never saw the final result, but Michael Bartley visited him just before his death with a swag of photographs to assure him that all was well with the old girl.

22

Back in the water

Thursday, 1 March 2018 was a very special day at the picturesque Bartley's Slipway at Woolwich on Sydney Harbour.

Just after 8 am, with the MV *Krait*'s reconditioned stern section poking proudly out over the water lapping into the boatshed on a rising tide, the newly repainted 84-year-old former Japanese fishing boat began a cautious slide back into her natural environment.

As the wake from passing Rivercat ferries and pleasure craft crashed into the marina between Cockatoo Island and Clarkes Point Reserve, and after 14 long months of being high and dry inside the shed undergoing a comprehensive reconditioning of her hull and decks, the *Krait* slipped quietly down a set of old tram rails on three cradles and back to the salt water of Sydney Harbour.

Michael Bartley cautiously coaxed the large electric winch that lowered the cradle and its record heavy load into the harbour, watched by his proud team of shipwrights, yard hands and a small group of onlookers. Australia's most acclaimed – but possibly least recognised – maritime war relic finally bobbed at the wharf.

As soon as she floated off the cradle, the shipwrights tied the *Krait* to the pier and mooring posts then scurried over her looking for any telltale leaks. With pumps at the ready, the old boat creaked and strained as she floated freely, working out the kinks of 14 months on the slips while the new joints in her hull began to swell and seal.

After several days tied up at Woolwich and with her interior as dry as a bone, Australia's most famous World War II 'warship' was towed back across the harbour, her bow high from lack of ballast, to the ANMM for the final restoration work to be undertaken on her 1943 configuration.

The *Krait* was due to be back on public view in time for the seventy-fifth anniversary of the raid on Singapore in September 2018. An enhanced display, including interpretive panels linked to digital material on the websites of both the AWM and the maritime museum, would tell the stories of the vessel, the 1943 Jaywick raid on Singapore, 'Z' Special Unit and the men who participated in the epic mission.

Had he been at Woolwich that sparkling autumn morning, Douglas Herps would surely have had a tear in his eye and a spring in his step to be witnessing the rebirth of the boat that he regarded as a solemn memorial to his mates. Here she was, back in the water and looking close to the way she had when she set sail northwards from Broken Bay 75 years earlier at the start of her extraordinary mission. His pet project was at last primed for the final phase.

During an episode of ABC TV's *Australian Story* Herps had made clear his vision for the boat. 'I'm very proud to have been a member of "Z", but whenever I start thinking about it – unfortunately you start thinking about your mates. And when I personally look at it [the *Krait*], I see mates of mine who were killed. We regard it as a war memorial. And that's what we want it to be. We do not appreciate what a wonderful mission this was, and it's got to be told, the story of the *Krait*.'

Like all veterans of the top-secret campaign waged against the Japanese, he took great pride in the success of Operation Jaywick even though no details had emerged until well after the war was won.

'There they were [Japanese forces], on top of the world. And suddenly there are ships blown up in their harbour. And they couldn't explain it and they were panic-stricken,' he said. 'To have achieved such a wonderful thing: you'd want to shout it from the rooftops, wouldn't you? And yet they never did. They never did.'

Even as Douglas Herps lay on his deathbed, he extracted promises of help from family and friends, media, captains of industry and political operators that they would see the *Krait* preservation project through to its conclusion.

The return of MV *Krait* from Bartley's slipway was a red-letter day for the team at the ANMM. As soon as she was tied up at the museum's wharf, work began on the next phase – transforming the vessel's fit-out back to the 1943 configuration, to show the general public the truly epic achievement of 14 men and a small, wooden boat.

For the then Chief of Army, now Chief of the Defence Force Lieutenant General Angus Campbell, the mission to have the *Krait* refurbished and restored is a personal one. Not only did the army provide $500,000 towards the work, but he regards the vessel as a tangible link to a pivotal moment in the development of special forces in Australia.

'It also speaks to a time of great decision internationally and for our nation's future during the Second World War, at a time when things were not going well and we were still struggling – but perhaps there was a possibility emerging for the Allied nations,' Campbell said. 'If we just pass it by and lose that history, we're losing a connection and an opportunity to take our young people [and] remind them that, with all of the extraordinary technology and with all of the possibilities of the modern era, it's the heart, the soul and the determination of the men and women of today; it's that that will make them special.

'There's no comfort; there's no easy life. This was a very physically demanding mission and I think it is extraordinarily valuable to be able to say, "This is what a special operation might require of you – and your nation is not seeking your service in comfort, it seeks it at the very edge of human capacity."'

Acknowledgments

I am deeply grateful for the tireless support and work of my wife, Verona Burgess, in the production of *The Mighty Krait*. As my editor and muse, she has once again nursed me through the process and polished a rough yarn into what we hope is an enthralling tale.

My daughter, Lucy, and stepkids, Daniel and Jenna, are always supportive and look out for their mum when I'm away.

This book, timed to coincide with the seventy-fifth anniversary of Operation Jaywick, had its genesis during a meeting I had at the Woolwich pub with Jonathan Herps and the late naval surveyor Warwick Thomson.

Jonathan's late father and 'Z' Special Unit veteran Douglas Herps was the power behind the 2017–18 restoration of the MV *Krait*. He started the ball rolling and convinced all the players of the merits of his vision for a permanent display.

Jonathan and his brother, Nicholas, have been enthusiastic supporters of their father's grand plan and this book.

The *Krait* belongs to the Australian War Memorial. To its director Brendan Nelson, former deputy director Tim Sullivan and the head of collections Brian Dawson, a sincere thank you for your backing and guidance. The former Chief of Army and now Chief of the Defence Force, Lieutenant General Angus Campbell, also gave generously of his time.

The old vessel is in the safe hands of the Australian National Maritime Museum. The director Kevin Sumption, his deputy Peter Rout, the curator of historic vessels David Payne and fleet manager Damien Allan provided invaluable assistance.

Fleet surveyor the late Warwick Thomson was a mine of information and a very enthusiastic advocate for the *Krait* and for this book.

A big thank you to Brian Young who was very generous in providing access to invaluable material from his collection and that of his late father, Jaywick operative and radio operator Horrie.

Despite his health problems, media commentator and former Labor powerbroker Graham Richardson has provided tireless backing to the restoration.

Michael Chaney was kind with his time, as was former New South Wales Liberal Party leader and keen military historian Peter Collins, as well as Jack Thurgar from the Commando Association.

A special thank you to Winsome Denyer and the team at ABC TV's *Australian Story* for the wonderful piece they made about Douglas Herps and the *Krait* preservation project.

Michael and Catriona Bartley were incredibly generous and provided unfettered access for my many visits to the *Krait* during the 14 months it spent on their slipway at Woolwich on Sydney Harbour. Michael's knowledge of the shipwright trade and old wooden boats was extremely important in the production of this book.

A big thank you to Brisbane-based film-maker John Schindler, who provided me with some terrific background material including his exclusive interview with Horrie Young for his documentary film *Tigers and Snakes*.

My thanks also to John and Francene Nobbs, Jim Truscott and Rick Moor for their unique perspectives and to Tony Crilly and his family for their kind assistance.

I pay tribute to the late journalist and author Ronald McKie and his invaluable book *The Heroes* (Angus&Robertson, 1960; 1994 edition Angus and Robertson, an imprint of Harper Collins*Publishers)*, which filled in many holes about Operation Jaywick. Mr McKie was also a wonderful personal inspiration to a young lad many, many years ago.

It was a great privilege to meet and interview the wonderful Moss Berryman.

All of my books feature as many 'live' quotes as possible, but where the participants are no longer with us I prefer to use their own written words contained in logs and diaries wherever possible, rather than paraphrasing.

The National Archives of Australia's digitised collection is an incredible resource and was vital in the production of this book, as were the collections of the Australian War Memorial, the RAN Seapower Centre and the Australian Army History Unit. I thank them for giving me permission to quote from the following crucial source documents: NAA: MP1185/8, 1932/2/85 – Report of operation 'Jaywick' carried out by MV *Krait* Sept–Oct 1943; NAA: A3269, E2/C – [Lower South China Sea, Singapore –] Diary/Log Book relating to Operation JAYWICK [Singapore] compiled by Lieutenant DMN Davidson, RNVR [Royal Navy Volunteer Reserve]; NAA A3269 [Lower South China Sea, Singapore –] JAYWICK Operation [Narrative] [Singapore]; and *The logbook of MV* Krait AWM 315419/017/003. Thanks too to the Australian National Maritime Museum for allowing me to use the *Draft Vessel Management Plan for MV* Krait.

Further suggested reading: the monograph *Krait: The Fishing Boat that went to War* by historians Lynette Ramsay Silver and Tom Hall (Sally Milner Publishing, 1992); and *Kill the Tiger*

236

(Dunshaulin Co, 2007) and *Operation Rimau* (Hachette Australia, 2015) by Peter Thompson and Robert Macklin.

Once again, I sincerely thank Catherine Milne, Nicola Robinson and the team at HarperCollins for their commitment to our stories and to Australian authors in general. Book publishing is a challenging business these days and CEO James Kellow and his staff are rising to it.

Many people are involved in the process of producing a book and if I have failed to mention anyone who assisted us with *The Mighty Krait* then please accept my apologies and my sincere thanks.

Donations to the MV *Krait* preservation fund can be made at: www.anmm.gov.au/Get-Involved/Donate

Ian McPhedran
Sydney 2018

Index